ABSOLUTELY ABBY'S
101 JOB SEARCH SECRETS

A CORPORATE RECRUITER HANDS
YOU THE KEYS TO YOUR
JOB SEARCH SUCCESS

ABBY KOHUT

Absolutely yours!
Abby

Edited by:
Debbi Stumpf
Peggy Morrissey

Cover Design and Interior Layout by:
Ken Kohut

Front Cover "Keys" Illustration:
©2008 Viktoriya Yatskina

ISBN-13: 9781450578424 – ISBN-10: 145057842X

Acknowledgements

I gratefully thank all of the jobseekers that have given me the opportunity thus far to provide them with weekly words of wisdom as Absolutely Abby. Your feedback and trust gives me the daily motivation to continue to find news ways to guide you.

I thank Mark Victor Hansen for creating the Mega Book Seminar, which inspired me to set the author that I have had inside me for years, free.

Abundant thank yous to Barbara De Angelis for developing the mantra "The World Is Waiting for Your Words". The world didn't have to wait too long, thanks to you.

Thank you to Debbi Stumpf for your thoughts, your incredible strength, your friendship, and your infinite wisdom. I could write an entire book about the gifts you offer to this world – and someday, I just might. Together we will accomplish great things. It is my honor to know you. Thank you for being my editor and publicist.

Thank you to Dr. Ilana Zablozki-Amir for helping to keep my mind, my spirit, and my body healthy so I can inspire others. I have always been proud to call you my friend.

Thanks to Mark Victor Hansen and Robert Allen for writing "Cash In a Flash". Thanks to my Abundance Alliance Group – you are a bunch of amazing women who help to keep me on track.

Thank you to Keith Bogen for continuing to teach us all the power of networking.

Thanks to Ellen DeGeneres. While we have never met, you have kept me laughing for so many years, especially during the rough patches. Your desire to help the world has rubbed off on so many people and continues to inspire me to greatness. As your biggest fan, I look forward to the day when I will be able to thank you in person.

Ken, I saved you for last, because you are the BEST, and because you are why "Absolutely Abby" began. Without your love, support, encouragement, and patience, I would not be able to accomplish half of what I do. You are the best life partner I could have ever asked for. I look forward to achieving my career dreams with you by my side.

Foreword

Become the captain of your own ship...

Recruiting is not a science. If it were a college course, it would be part of the psychology curriculum. Being an effective recruiter requires a strong amount of insight and the ability to "read" people, but recruiters are born from a myriad of backgrounds.

As you continue on your journey, you will hear a variety of opinions from different recruiters, coaches, and Human Resources professionals surrounding each detail of the job search process. With all these choices, whose opinion is correct?

Take, for example, the one-page resume debate. If you surveyed 100 recruiters, how many do you think would believe that your resume should be one page? The answer is probably, a handful. If you asked the same group about a two-page resume and a three-page resume, you would find many different opinions as well.

As for the cover letter debate, some recruiters find them valuable, while others do not. Some believe that you should send one out regardless, while others say that they don't read them, so you might as well not bother.

What is a jobseeker supposed to do when faced with all this insanity? How is a person supposed to decide what to do?

The answer is actually quite simple. The most important opinion that matters is YOURS. Your goal should be to take in all the information that you can, and to organize it in such a way that you can analyze the results. Then, choose what makes the most sense for you. That will be the right answer.

However, please use common sense. If someone tells you that it's OK to chew gum in an interview or that it's OK to wear flip-flops and a T-shirt on an interview with a company that has a casual dress code, think twice about following that person's advice.

In your job search, you are the captain of your ship. You get to decide how to do things, when to do things, and if to do things at all. Always consider multiple opinions before you decide what to do. But, the right opinion will always be your own, because deep down inside, you always know what's right for you.

Drawn from my 15 years of experience and research in recruiting and Human Resources, this book is intended to provide insight into what corporate recruiters and Human Resource professionals look for when they are evaluating your qualifications. Simply reading this book will not guarantee you success. However, consistently applying the strategies mentioned, as well as developing your own personal interview style, will greatly enhance your chances of victory amidst the competition. I wish you the best of luck with your search as you begin to take charge of your career!

Abby Kohut
President & Lead Consultant
Staffing Symphony, LLC

Are you ready for a Career Wake Up Call?

Looking back at your life, can you think of an experience that, at the time, left you feeling sad, depressed, or hopeless, yet which ended up being a blessing in disguise? In my case it happened twice.

It was December 1996. I was working for a software company and thought I had it all. I managed to land my first job in recruiting with barely any experience under my belt. I had an office with a window and a yummy cafeteria in the building with a heaping salad bar. I was interviewing 10 people a day and, within a year and a half, had hired 525 of them, effectively doubling the size of the company. I was on cloud ten.

Then one day…BOOM! The world came crashing down. This wonderful company with its fast-paced entrepreneurial culture was swallowed up by a giant in the industry. Life as I knew it was over. Jobs were eliminated and reorganized as the BIG company moved in. In short, what used to be a happy place turned completely upside down. I left through the open door with only my memories.

Rather than dwelling on what could have been, I thought about my next career move and what it should be. I loved helping people's dreams come true, not just by finding them a job, but by finding them the "right" job. This was the inspiration, which drove me to create my first company Career Dreams, whose mission was to help people discover their ideal job.

Eventually I decided to go back to corporate America to gain more experience and to add skills to my portfolio. There was yet another BOOM in 2005 when the second company I thought I would retire with sent the majority of my department packing. At the time, I didn't realize that what seemed like a swift kick was actually a Career Wake Up Call. Without that BOOM, I would not have become a Staffing Consultant and would not have had the opportunity to meet all of you, much less write this book.

It took lots of time and plenty of hard work, but today, I am finally living my career dream. Through my blogs, tele-seminars, speaking engagements and this book, I have the opportunity to reach hundreds of people like you, in various stages of career transition. The people I have met while networking and the stories I have heard have enhanced my ability to help people find the right job as a Consultant. I answered my call and I'm now ready to dedicate my life to helping other people answer theirs as Absolutely Abby.

Take a step back and look at your current circumstance. Have you answered your Career Wake Up Call? Are you in a profession and industry that you Absolutely love, or did your career just happen to you? Are you ready to show the world your talents like never before? Is there a business you've secretly wanted to start? Is there a product you've wanted to market? Is there a career dream that is still unfulfilled?

Instead of just searching for jobs, search for career opportunities that make you jump out of bed in the morning. Apply for positions that will inspire you to produce great work, whether your boss is watching you or not. Seek to find a job that engulfs you in passion. Answer your Career Wake Up Call today. Let me show you how...

Searching for a Job That You Love

▪ 1 ▪   Designing a Career Vision Board

Although experts may have varying viewpoints as to the exact methodologies involved, leading motivational speakers and authors tend to agree on one fact: if you can see it and believe it, it will happen. No concept could be more appropriate for job seekers.

In her daily motivational blog, Jennifer Scott from HireEffect LLC says, "If you write down what you want, you have the start of your plan, and the basis for your goal-setting. Draft your dream job description, the whole thing...responsibilities, compensation, location...all of it. Then, write your offer letter, and sign it to accept." Moreover, Jennifer believes that adding pictures of your ideal job improves the visualization. Select pictures of your future office décor or pictures of your potential customers for the greatest impact. You may even want to create a mock business card with your new title on it. In other words, create a "career vision board".

This concept goes hand-in-hand with an exercise that I have offered to jobseekers for years. On the left side of a piece of paper, jot down the specific tasks that you love to engage in at work. Then, write the tasks that you procrastinate doing for as long as possible, or strongly dislike doing, on the right side. Your goal should be to target your search towards jobs that are filled with a majority of responsibilities from the left side of your page – the tasks you love.

This exercise, like a workout program you use to stay trim, won't benefit you unless you actually do it. While it may seem trivial, you will see how helpful it can be when you are developing and honing your search plan.

Accept the challenge – do this exercise right now or schedule some time later when you can focus 100% of your attention on it. You may find if

1

you are completely honest with yourself that you actually know what your ideal job looks like. Once you have a clear picture of it on paper, you'll find reviewing it will put you back on track on those days where disappointments outnumber your successes.

> **Absolutely Abby's Advice:** *Starting your search without first clarifying your goals is like getting on a rollercoaster that hasn't finished being constructed. To land in your ideal job, you first have to know exactly what it looks like. The clearer the vision, the better the actions and the choices you'll make along the way to finding your career dream.*

▪ 2 ▪ Strengthening your Strengths

Let your strengths do the talking while your weaknesses do the walking!

One of my favorite motivational speakers is Marcus Buckingham, the co-author of "Now, Discover Your Strengths". In the book, the authors explain that managers are generally instructed to complete performance appraisals for their employees based on their strengths and weaknesses. Typical performance review meetings include ten minutes about the employee's successes in the past year, and the rest of the time is devoted to a conversation about how the employee can improve their weaknesses by taking classes or completing "stretch assignments".

The authors believe, instead, that employees are much more likely to be successful when they are encouraged to take on more responsibilities that involve their strengths. During reviews they say, managers should discuss their employee's weaknesses only briefly, and then re-focus their attention on potential projects in areas in which they can excel and also enjoy. This, they say, will result in a much more productive, efficient, and satisfied employee.

When you're searching for your next position, make every effort to avoid jobs with responsibilities that you would rather pull your hair out piece by piece than do. At the same time, try to think of the responsibilities from jobs you've had that you love so much that you would do them for free. Then, search for positions with those types of responsibilities.

For example, if you are an Executive Assistant and you love working with spreadsheets in Excel, search for positions supporting a CFO or a Vice President of Sales. If you detest scheduling flight arrangements, choose a company that only has employees in one location, rather than spread all over the country. If you love to be busy and take on extra projects, choose a smaller company that relies on its associates to wear numerous hats.

Think about strengths in terms of sports. Let's say your son tells you this summer that he wants to try baseball, soccer, and football, all at once, and you begrudgingly agree. You take out a second mortgage on your house to pay for these activities and then sign him up. All of sudden, your son starts exhibiting skills on par with Reggie Jackson, and wants to do nothing but play baseball, eat and sleep (and occasionally go to the movies). Would you encourage him to continue to play football and soccer if he was the subject of frequent ribbing by his teammates, or would you pay for baseball lessons so that he could hone his skills? Personally, I would buy him a new bat and glove and get him ready for spring training.

> ***Absolutely Abby's Advice:*** *Spend the time that you have now to really get clear on what you want your next career move to be. This is the perfect time to expand your horizons and think outside the box. What responsibilities have you loved that you also excelled at? What have you wanted to do more of that you haven't had the chance to yet? What business would you start if you didn't need lots of money to do it? The answers to these questions will help you take charge and re-evaluate how to make your career dreams come true.*

▪ 3 ▪   One Size Doesn't Fit All

In order to love your job, you have to love ALL of the components of the job, and not JUST the job itself. Let me explain…

In order for a job to be perfectly suited for you, it has to be perfectly suited in many ways. You have to have a wonderful boss in a wonderful company with the ideal culture for you. Your schedule has to be exactly what you'd like it to be and you have to have the exact amount of work/life balance that you desire. And, your job must be situated in an appropriately sized company as this can also affect your happiness.

A jobseeker once sent me this e-mail, "While my prior experience has been working with large companies, I have been interviewing recently with smaller companies, and have been getting resistance because of the perception that my large company experience hasn't prepared me for the "fast pace" or the diversity of work experience of a much smaller company. How can I get past these misconceptions?"

What I explained to the jobseeker is that many recruiters believe that there is, in fact, a major difference between smaller entrepreneurial companies and larger, more established companies. This difference cannot be ignored when trying to match a candidate to an open position.

Let's look at small companies first. Many small companies provide opportunities to take on more responsibilities within your job, because there are not as many employees who are qualified to do those tasks. Sometimes you take on projects that you have absolutely no idea how to complete, but because you are smart, you are asked to do them anyway. Small company employees may work longer hours because they are in their start-up and fast-paced phase, which means deadlines are abundant. Small companies may offer lower salaries but may be flexible enough to offer promotions and raises, throughout the year, for excellent performance.

Larger companies offer long-term career paths since there are usually plenty of steps between you and the CEO. Navigating the career ladder may be tricky though, because your peers tend to be vying for similar roles. Large companies typically offer generous benefits including healthcare, tuition reimbursement, and flexible, substantial paid time off plans. Some even offer daycare or adoption assistance. Until recently, large companies also offered a sense of stability and permanence, although these days, the only thing that is permanent is your network.

If you want to make the transition from large company experience to a smaller, entrepreneurial company, it's up to you to explain to a recruiter or hiring manager why your big company experience is relevant. Come to the interview armed with details about the relevant accomplishments that you have that can match the pace or the operational details needed by a smaller company. Explain that your big company experience can help the start-up or non-profit grow, because you can teach them how larger, more successful companies accomplish certain processes.

If working at a small company is a top priority for you, volunteer for a non-profit organization while you're searching to show that you can handle fast-paced entrepreneurial responsibilities with few resources. This will give you a good taste of what it's really like in comparison to working in a big company. Then you can make a better decision as to which size company you prefer.

If you're trying to go in the other direction, from small company to large, you should have an easier time. However, the recruiters will want to hear reasons other than, "I want great benefits" or "I want stability". Be prepared to explain why you will not feel stifled when you are only permitted to work on your own specific assignments because everything else is "someone else's job".

> **Absolutely Abby's Advice:** *Making the decision on whether to be a big fish in a small bowl or a small fish in a big one is critical to your job satisfaction. No job will be 100% perfect for you. However, if you strive to get as close to perfection as possible, without settling when times seem difficult, you will find happiness even if there are small imperfections along the way. And when you love your job, the imperfections are not nearly as bad as you might have thought they once were.*

▪ 4 ▪ Industry Daydreaming

As important as it is to choose the ideal job, it is also important to choose the ideal industry that is a match for your personality and work ethic.

I Absolutely love the entertainment industry. Nothing would make me happier than to be involved with the comings and goings of the stars. I'd practically consider working for free for the chance to be in their daily presence. I also love many spectator sports. Doing some consulting work for Major League Baseball or the United States Tennis Association is a dream of mine. And then there are little furry creatures. If the Bronx Zoo was hiring recruiters, I'd be the first on line. That's me. What about you?

One day soon, I am quite sure that you will be presented with a job offer. While you may not want to be seen as picky or high maintenance, you Absolutely must consider the consequences of your choices. Choosing the right job in the wrong industry can still turn into a blemish on your resume.

Some industries offer fast-paced cultures with lots of deadlines. Take Wall Street for example. Working in that environment requires a strong work ethic and a no nonsense attitude. Then there is the IT world – every employee works with strict deadlines to keep up with changing technology. If you choose the healthcare, non-profit, or education industries, you will find that most employees there are on a mission to make a difference in the world.

As a consultant, I have had the privilege of wearing a variety of hats in many different worlds. I have explored IT, education, the non-profit world, pharmaceuticals, healthcare, manufacturing, and publishing. I managed to enjoy them all, because I saw the benefits of each while I was experiencing them. But not everyone's work personality is that flexible. It's important to choose wisely now, to avoid needing to search again next year because you made the wrong choice.

Knowing the industries you are interested in will enable you to create more specific companies to target in your search. Mentioning your specific industries of interest will also help you develop more memorable connections at networking events.

> *Absolutely Abby's Advice:* *Make it your mission to find the ideal job in the ideal industry. If you cannot find an exact match right now, make sure to craft a plan as to how to get there in the future. When you love what you do, it no longer seems like work, and that should be the ultimate goal for each and every one of you.*

▪ 5 ▪   Sweep Your Way to the Top

I'm dating myself by saying that "The Secret of My Success" was one of my favorite childhood movies, but it's a risk that I'm willing to take. In the movie, Michael J. Fox plays a character that uses his creativity and ingenuity to work his way to the top of the company. The great part about it is that he starts his climb as a mailroom clerk.

We all daydream about the company we'd love to work for. We idealize the industry and the people in it. All industries have their merits, but some are more glamorous and interesting to dream about. In my career, I've been fortunate enough to have gained experience in many different industries. They all have their pluses and minuses, but my experiences have created the substance of who I am today.

As I previously mentioned, the one industry I have yet to experience, which is on the tippy-top of my list, is the entertainment industry. I continue to dream about moving to LA to take on a recruiting project for a major motion picture or cable network. If the stars were all aligning perfectly, I will be working for Ellen DeGeneres some day soon.

It's fun to dream, but at some point you need to take action. Consider one or more of the following options:

- ✓ Volunteer for the organization that you wish you could work for, or volunteer for an organization that your favorite companies support. Then, use your networking skills to make good connections.

- ✓ Apply for positions that are one level down from yours, and prove that you belong at the higher level by excelling at your job within the first six months.

- ✓ Sign up with temporary agencies and accept assignments in companies that you might consider working for. Then, be the best temporary worker that the company has ever seen, and they may never want to let you go.

- ✓ Last, but not least, consider consulting or working part-time for your favorite companies. Superstars are frequently converted to regular employees.

> **Absolutely Abby's Advice:** *If you find a way to "sweep the floor" at your favorite company as well as Michael J. Fox delivered mail, only good things can happen to you. Creativity will be the Secret of Your Success — today more than ever! And by the way... if you hear that Ellen DeGeneres is hiring, please give me a call.*

▪ 6 ▪   Try It – You Just Might Like It

In recent years, companies have employed different methods to hire talent, especially in recessed economies. Some companies offer deferred start dates to employees, some offer stronger benefit plans in lieu of competitive salaries, and still others simply delay their offers for a quarter or two. Lately, temporary, contracting, and consulting opportunities have become much more commonplace, because they enable companies to avoid paying large amounts of money for benefits, and they can also delay their hiring decisions.

There are many good reasons to consider searching for and accepting a temporary or consulting assignment. Here are some of them:

Temporary assignments typically involve a shorter interview process

Companies are less likely to require many interview rounds for temporary positions because they can easily end your assignment without notice. This enables you to get your foot in the door at a new company relatively quickly. Once you are in, it's time to shine like you have never shined before. Make every effort to complete your work before it is due, even if you have to work on your own time to do it. But, be especially careful to monitor your quality, as that is what counts most.

A temporary assignment is a "try and buy" for you

How often did you wish that you could have seen inside a crystal ball before you accepted an offer? How many times have you wished that you knew the inside scoop about the company and the manager before you made a decision to spend the next 3-5 years at the company? Enter the temporary assignment! Voila – crystal ball!

<u>A temporary assignment doesn't have to be temporary</u>

I can't count the number of people that I know who have started out in consulting assignments that eventually became permanent. One of my friends signed up for a 3-month assignment in a Human Resources department, which later became a 12-month assignment, and then finally became a more permanent offer. Another friend of mine, in the IT field, networked her way into a consulting assignment with a top echelon clothing designer, and then received an offer after just 6 months. It happens more often than not…if you excel at what you do.

> **Absolutely Abby's Advice:** *Look at a temporary or consulting assignment as a wonderful opportunity to showcase your talents. Who knows? Perhaps you'll decide to become "permanently temporary" and become a professional consultant. Or, perhaps this "temporary" assignment just might grow into the ideal job that you have been waiting for all along. Regardless, enjoy the assignment as it is yet another experience to add to your portfolio.*

▪ 7 ▪ Straying From the Mothership

Being a new parent is clearly one of the biggest challenges there is. Choosing to go back to work may seem like an even bigger challenge, as you consider all the emotional and financial variables. As you begin your job search, make a list of things that you believe are requirements for your new job and a separate list of "nice to haves". Evaluating the questions listed below, *before* you begin your search, will help you stay on track and find a job that is perfectly suited for you and your family.

Work Schedule

Are you looking for a part-time or full-time job? What hours are you willing and/or able to work? Do you need to find a job that enables you to leave on time every day or is some overtime acceptable? If full-time, should your hours be 9-5, 8-4 or 7-3?

Time Off

How important is vacation and sick time? Does the company offer personal time so that when your child is ill, you don't have to take vacation days off? If your child is ill within the first six months, will you be able to take the time off, even if it's unpaid?

Career Growth or Stability

If you were in a high level, demanding position before you became a parent, are you ready to assume that level of responsibility again? Or, would you rather find a stable position that you enjoy, but one that does not require as much effort or attention outside the office?

Work Location

Do you need to find a job close to home? Should you look for jobs where you can telecommute daily or once a week?

Child Care

Have you found someone responsible to take care of your child so that you can be worry free once you get back to work and have the emotional & mental stamina that it requires?

Compensation

How important is the compensation offered for the position? Should your salary be equal to or above the cost of daycare, or are you simply going back to work for personal career development? Does the position need to come with benefits?

<u>Interviewing Skills</u>

Are you ready to start interviewing or are you a bit rusty? Do you have someone available to help point out your blind spots? Are you confident that you have prepared your answers to the more difficult questions?

> **Absolutely Abby's Advice:** *When going back to work, there are so many variables to consider. Only after you have answered the questions above, and any other ones that you come up with, will you then be really ready to start on your job search journey. Then, muster all of your newfound mommy or daddy confidence and begin the search for your brand new career!*

▪ 8 ▪   A Pocketbook Full of Lessons

On a recent Father's Day, I spent quite a bit of time thinking about my dad and the lessons I learned from him at a young age. Dad was a traditionalist. He had a single job for his entire career and ended up retiring from it at age 65. If there is such a thing as an "entrepreneurial gene" I clearly inherited it from my mother. Despite our differences, the lessons that dad taught me about the working world still ring true today.

My father was a production manager for a family-owned handbag factory. I can still remember the smell of the leather samples that he brought home, much to my mother's delight. Besides handbags, dad brought home a variety of stories about his employees, from which I learned these five basic principles of career success:

1) Pursue a career that you are not only skilled at, but also enjoy doing five days a week. If you are like the many people who still aren't sure where your passions lie, seriously consider taking a career assessment test like the Strong Interest Inventory, the

Strengths Finder, or the Myers-Briggs. My dad loved being a production manager and especially loved the manufacturing industry. He was in the right place in the right time.

2) Pursue an industry in which there is a need for the products and services today, and where there will be equal if not more demand in the future. Even if you don't expect to stay at one company for 30 years, make sure that there will be plenty of other choices of companies in your industry as times goes on. Handbags are here to stay. They never go out of style because we women can never have enough of them. This also holds true for shoes and clothes and make-up. Need I say more?

3) Develop a craft and become an expert at it. Although my dad obviously was not a big fan of change, he was a prime target for opportunities at other handbag manufacturing companies. These days, he would have received calls from headhunters all the time trying to steal him away from his company, which would have offered him great promotional opportunities.

4) Network with others in your industry. I remember dad attending national conferences to perfect his craft. From the other attendees and presenters, dad honed his skills and also came back with information on the latest developments in his industry, to share with the owner of the company.

5) Be committed. I'm not talking about being committed to one company for your entire career. I am talking about being committed to whatever you are doing at the time. It means taking responsibility for your achievements and for the quality and quantity of work that you produce.

> *Absolutely Abby's Advice:* *Times are different now than they were even just ten short years ago. You cannot rely on your boss or your company to manage your career — you have to rely on yourself, your mentors and your coaches. Take the time to really hone your craft and to build your network. That is when true career success really begins.*

▪ 9 ▪   Career Passion in The Big City

Inspiring people are everywhere, just like networking connections. You just have to keep your eyes open and start noticing them.

I was born in Brooklyn and will always consider myself a New Yorker. We're different kinds of birds but ultimately we all have a multitude of interesting stories, thanks to the Big Apple. My favorite ones are about the people who love their jobs.

I don't remember when I first noticed Tom, my favorite subway conductor, but I have literally been talking about him for years. For those of you who have never taken a New York City subway, I highly recommend it. It's just like it appears on TV. You are smooshed like sardines half the time, and constantly make attempts to avoid crashing into your neighbor. The other half the time, you're people watching, and boy, do we have interesting people to watch.

Tom is one of the first people that helped me understand what loving your job looks like. The subway conductor's job is to announce the next station, to make sure that everyone is safely getting in and out of the train, and then to say, "please stand clear of the closing doors". Ah...I can just hear it now.

Tom goes way beyond the norm. He announces the weather and the time every few minutes. He also mentions the tourist attractions at each stop. He tells us about the Empire State Building, Times Square, Carnegie Hall and Wall Street to name a few. He also tells us what's going on that day if he knows of any local events. He's more like a tour guide than a conductor. One day when leaving the train, I decided to thank Tom for making my ride such a pleasure and to encourage him to keep going. He smiled as if to say, "I'm glad you noticed." Tom clearly loves his job because he goes way beyond the job requirements to help passengers actually enjoy their New York City subway commute.

My favorite New Jersey Transit bus driver named Dave loves his job as well. As we leave New York City, he typically gives us the weather for the next day along with the traffic report for the commute home, and finishes with the interesting news in the media. He concludes his five-minute speech with, "OK. Let's go home." What an Absolute pleasure to have these people in our life. They add a spice of life to our mundane, daily activities because they love what they do.

Imagine how you would act if you loved what you did. Would you smile more? Would you prance around the office? Would you offer to get involved in projects, rather than groaning when someone hands you more work? Would you become the welcome wagon for new employees? Would you go above and beyond and launch your career farther and faster because of it? I believe so.

> ***Absolutely Abby's Advice:*** *As tempting as it is to accept a job offer when you receive it, spend plenty of time contemplating the opportunity before you make a decision. If this is not a job that you are sure you will love, consider if waiting for the right one to surface is a viable alternative. Finding a job that you love is worth all the time you put in to find it. Only then will you feel the complete range of career satisfaction.*

Rockin' Resumes & Creative Cover Letters

▪ 10 ▪   Truth or Consequences

Don't lie to your mom about breaking her favorite vase, and don't lie on your resume either!

In one episode of the TV series "The Brady Bunch", Peter Brady wanted to go on a camping trip more than anything else in the world. He had all of his gear packed, and couldn't wait to experience the calm of the great outdoors with all of his friends. And then it happened…he broke his mom's favorite vase while he was playing ball in the house after his mother told him not to. Those of you who are devout Brady Bunch fans know the moral of this story. Although Peter lied and claimed innocence, he later confessed and had to pay the consequences by canceling his camping trip.

Lying during your job search process can have similarly disastrousconsequences.

Your resume is a written version of you. It is a document explaining who you are and the roles you have played in the past. Although it is not necessarily a legal document, it becomes a component of your personnel file once you are hired. When you fill out a job application, which IS a legal document, recruiters will compare the two to ensure that they match exactly. Some companies also compare both documents to your information on LinkedIn.

Companies take lying seriously. Even if it seems like a small fib such as an inflated salary or incorrect months of employment, it may still hamper your chances for success. Like Peter, some people get caught lying at the eleventh hour – either right before they receive an offer, right before their start date, or worse yet, six months after they start. In some cases, companies discover these indiscretions years later by accident, during an

17

audit, and due to corporate policy make the decision to terminate the employees who lied. It just isn't a good business decision to lie on your resume or application.

A fellow recruiter shared another example with me about a person, who was obviously not a Brady Bunch fan. She was conducting a job search for an Executive Assistant to a CFO. One day the perfect candidate on paper, who I'll call Alice, walked into her office. Alice's resume listed her five roles as an Executive Assistant in top firms reporting to C-level associates. She had a college degree, extracurricular leadership experiences, and top-notch computer skills. Her references were impeccable, and she was hired immediately. She was adored by the CFO by everyone else on her team, and by the other Executive Assistants in the company.

Several weeks into her tenure, Alice became friendly with one of her teammates and started casually chatting about her past. She confided in the wrong person and told the person that she had fabricated her entire resume, and that her references were actually her friends pretending to be former managers. Alice was immediately asked to pack her bags, with security and everyone else watching, despite the phenomenal job she was doing.

> **Absolutely Abby's Advice:** *While comparing Peter Brady's vase incident to the real world may seem farfetched, the moral here is 100% true. Lying about breaking your mom's favorite vase, or about the details of your resume, never results in a positive outcome. Honor your career and learn to explain the hiccups along the way. If Peter Brady decided to tell the truth, so can you.*

▪ 11 ▪   Shattering the One Page Rule

Probably one of the greatest debates between Human Resources professionals, headhunters, and hiring managers alike, is that of the one page resume. Some believe it is Absolutely essential to keep your resume to one page, while others believe it is an old wives' tale.

When you are graduating from high school or college, a one page resume is usually the best choice. Unless you have won a bunch of awards and also participated in a plethora of extracurricular activities before age 21, you should be able to fit a summary of your entire life on one page. This also holds true for those people who have held a single job for a long time and are beginning to search for new opportunities.

If you can fit everything you need to say onto one clean page, there's no need to stretch it out onto two. But, as many candidates find, after a few jobs you'll have lots to say and may choose to use two pages (or more).

Here are some reasons why a multi-page resume is ideal:

1) If you are not confined to one page, you will not have to use the teeny tiny fonts that someone, who left their magnifying glass home, will be unable to read.

2) You will have more room to add a section to each job experience entitled "Accomplishments" where you will be able to tell us why you excelled at your job rather than just doing it.

3) You will have room to add a sentence or two about your volunteer and extracurricular activities, explaining what skills you gained from these experiences.

4) You will have room to add a summary of your background or list of key skills representing your talents at the top of your resume.

5) You will have room to add things about you that might be interesting to an employer beyond your job, such as winning a softball tournament.

If you surveyed recruiters and Human Resources professionals, a small percentage will tell you that you need to stick to one page but the majority will advise you to cap it at two with three being the absolute maximum. I believe that it should be as long as it needs to be to explain your qualifications to your audience.

And my resume you ask? Not only did I break the one page rule, I shattered it. I have 20+ years of relevant work experience and loads of volunteer activities and memberships. My resume is filled with four pages that I am proud of, which make me a well-qualified Human Resources professional. I would never even try to fit my whole career on one page.

> **Absolutely Abby's Advice:** *The answer to whether your particular resume should be one page is like many other things in job searching…it depends. If you have a handful of work experience and great accomplishments to communicate, do not feel that you must confine yourself to just one page. Quality is far more important than quantity, in my humble opinion.*

▪ 12 ▪   E-Mail and Voicemail Conundrums

Regardless of the economy, one principle holds true with recruiters on all edges of the earth – you only have a few seconds to make a first impression. This applies to interviews, phone screens, e-mails and most of all, resumes.

What you do on the weekends and evenings with your friends, and how you communicate with one another, is clearly not a recruiter's concern. However, it becomes our concern when it spills into your work persona.

If you have an e-mail address called disco_king@yahoo.com or fun_lover@gmail.com, I implore you to create a new address that indicates a higher level of professionalism. Choose an e-mail address that is as close to your name as possible. For example, johndoe@yahoo.com is better than jdoe@yahoo.com. Why? Because it's easier for a recruiter and your networking connections to remember.

While we're on the topic of professionalism, pretend that you are a recruiter and call yourself on both your cell phone and home phone number. Listen to your voicemail message. Does it scream of intelligence, maturity, energy, and passion? If not, re-record it immediately. For those of you who have a song playing before your voicemail starts, choose a song that is professional, regardless of whether you personally like it. You are never going to be listening to it anyway so it's more important that it does not send a recruiter running for the hills. Opting for music without words is the best bet. Stay away from songs such as "Love Shack" or "My Girl Wants to Party All the Time".

> **Absolutely Abby's Advice:** *When you are searching for a job, anything and everything that you do is being evaluated. Choosing an unprofessional e-mail name and having an unprofessional voicemail may indicate a lack of judgment to some, a lack of responsibility to others, and a lack of maturity to the rest. There will be plenty of time for you to show your true personality once you have had some time to acclimate to your new company. As usual with job seeking, patience is a virtue!*

▪ 13 ▪ Your Ten Seconds of Fame

At some point in your job search you may have wondered why so many career experts spend lots of time talking about how to write the perfect resume, when you may have also heard that recruiters spend very little time reviewing it. The Absolute truth is that your resume has only about 10 seconds to really impress a recruiter, or it's likely to just go unnoticed.

Because of the volume of resumes we recruiters receive in response to an ad, it is our goal to quickly chisel down the pile to make it more manageable. Thus, your resume must present your information quickly, clearly, and in a way that makes your experience relevant to the position in question. In other words, your resume must be concise, powerful, and persuasive, all at the same time. If the recruiter can't figure out how your experience applies to the available position, your resume is not doing its job.

Let's try an experiment.

Pretend you are a recruiter trying to fill a position that you know you are very well suited for. Give yourself only ten seconds to review your resume. Does your resume give you a good understanding of your work experience? Do your qualifications shine through within those ten seconds? Do your accomplishments jump off the page? Do you have paragraphs or large chunks of information that act as "speed bumps" that slow you down as you scan through it?

When the ten seconds are over, consider editing your resume to reflect what you learned. Now might be a good time to blast those paragraphs into a few crisp, concise, focused bullets that can effectively tell the same story. Each bullet should be two lines at most, but one line is often sufficient. Short, powerful bullets give us reasons to keep reading. Consider showing your new resume to someone in the same industry or to someone with a similar job function to see if they believe that you have solved the ten second conundrum.

Last but not least, remember to proofread your newly edited resume. And, ask at least two friends who are strong writers to proofread it as well. The last thing you want is a well-formatted resume with excellent content to have grammar or spelling mistakes.

> ***Absolutely Abby's Advice:*** *With only ten seconds of fame, you need to work hard to get a recruiter's attention. Creating a concise resume will not only help you impress us on paper, but it will also help you become a focused interviewee who is able to answer questions as targeted as a speeding bullet.*

▪ 14 ▪ The Key to Keywords

Remember the time your parents first took you on a hayride? Round and round you went, watching the horse drawn carriage with glee as you looked forward to picking out the perfect pumpkin for carving. Haystacks are fun – except when it's your resume that's hidden like a needle in the stack. Using the right keywords will ensure that your needle rises to the surface and gets noticed.

These days, in addition to LinkedIn and other social media, most companies are using "applicant tracking systems" or job board search engines to find and source candidates. This means that the content of your resume is far more important than the way it is formatted. I still remember the glorious days of the pink and yellow-colored documents that came in the mail, one whose owner actually added a dab of cologne to it. In some cases, the recruiter won't know what your resume actually looks like until you're planted firmly in the chair across from their desk. So, while it is still important that your resume appears professional, your first goal is to make sure it gets unearthed in their search.

A company's haystack of resumes is their applicant tracking system. Although you may think it's a recruiter's job to find you, it's actually YOUR job to make yourself "findable". The more you help the recruiter, the faster they will find you and stop searching for your less than perfect competitors. How can you make your resume jump right out of the haystack? You guessed it – it's those pesky keywords! Do not underestimate how important they are. They can make you and they can definitely break you.

A creative way to determine the most important keywords to have on your resume is to pretend you are a recruiter who is searching for you. Without looking at your resume, take 5 minutes to brainstorm and write down the 20-40 keywords that you think should be included. Review your resume and highlight the keywords you find while you cross each off your list. Then, find a way to weave any leftover keywords into your resume. Try the same brainstorming session with a friend who is in the same industry or who has the same kind of job. You'll end up with twice as many keywords in addition to a new job search buddy.

Be sure to spell keywords correctly and avoid abbreviations of words that you want to be searchable. For example: If you are "proficient in Word and Excel", say that you are "proficient in Microsoft Word & Microsoft Excel." The same goes for Office vs. Microsoft Office. A recruiter cannot search on the words "office", "word" or "excel" because they are too common on a resume – people *excel* at their jobs, work in an *office*, and type 40 *words* a minute. Recruiters add "Microsoft" to their searches to make them more effective.

Demonstrating your "tech-knowledgy" on your resume will also help us find you, especially if you are an IT professional. Omitting the appropriate technical keywords from your profile is akin to having coffee without the mug. Be sure to list the software that you are proficient in along with the current version numbers. As you know, in the IT world, excelling at version 3.0, when the rest of the world is on 5.0 can be troublesome. Listing your tech-knowledgy (and spelling everything correctly) is one of the ways to guarantee an appearance of your resume during an electronic search.

A career coach once recommended to job seekers that they add a bunch of extra keywords on their resumes in a white font, so that they appear to be invisible. If you cannot figure out where these words belong on your resume, they should be invisible, literally. In other words, they should not be listed on your resume in the first place. If your resume gets scanned into an applicant tracking system, those sneaky white keywords will re-appear on the bottom of your resume in a strange looking list, and will no longer be invisible. Once a recruiter figures out that you were trying to be deceptive, you'll have at least one strike against you. You don't need any extra strikes against you, regardless of the job market.

> **Absolutely Abby's Advice:** *Keywords are a key to your success as an applicant. By cleverly weaving appropriate keywords into your resume, you can gain an edge over other candidates. But be sure to only list skills on your resume that you truly have. Honesty is the first step towards winning the race against your competition.*

▪ 15 ▪ Dashing to Perfection

David Silverman on the "Harvard Business Publishing" website wrote an article entitled, "How to Write a Résumé That Doesn't Annoy People". David writes, "Personally, I look at the width of the dashes. Microsoft Word will helpfully attempt to make a hyphen, n-dash, or m-dash based on the spacing you use when writing. Many people don't know this, and they don't notice that their dashes are all different lengths." (- versus – for example). David continues to say, "If you don't know that your own résumé is inconsistent, how can you be expected to supervise a multi-million dollar project?"

As picky as this seems, David is Absolutely correct! It is important to be detail oriented for many professions. For example, let's look at a Project Manager whose main objective is to manage the people and resources necessary to bring the project to successful completion under budget. Since the Project Manager bears the responsibility of overall project completion, he or she is also responsible for correcting the human errors that occur during the timeline. Many projects involve a writing component. That is, the project results must be summarized, and/or a presentation must be delivered, and/or documentation must be written. If the Project Manager cannot find his or her own errors, someone else is going to have to find them, which requires double work. So why would we hire someone whose work we are going to have to correct when instead, we can hire someone who is going to save us time by finding their own errors themselves?

Let's look at Administrative Assistants. When I am searching for a candidate to fill this role, does it matter to me whether the person has extra spaces between words (Type   40WPM versus Type 40WPM)? You bet! I credit my insane ability to catch these teeny tiny flaws to my English teachers in high school. Having to rewrite papers in those days seemed especially annoying, I must say. But, thanks to my early training, I taught myself to catch these little nitty-gritty typos before my teachers did. And, so have many other well-trained recruiters.

If you are not a detail-oriented writer, consider looking for positions that you can be successful in without that skill. Certain kinds of customer service and sales positions immediately come to mind, but there are many others. If you choose a position that highlights your strengths, you can easily rise to the top of your field, without having to be reminded at each performance review about your lack of detail-oriented writing.

> ***Absolutely Abby's Advice:*** *To be successful in a detail-oriented job, you need to be someone who thrives on perfecting the little details and catching mistakes for your boss, rather than the other way around…now that would be a great reason to hire you!*

▪ 16 ▪ Mind the Gap

There was a time in my career when seeing gaps on a candidate's resume raised a red flag. Once 9/11 happened, that concern flew out the window. The year that followed 9/11 was a time when even the best employees were being laid off due to no fault of their own. The years following 9/11 have presented similar challenges.

Any recruiter who doesn't understand a gap in your employment in the past several years should be reported to the Human Resources police (ah…if there only was such an organization).

One way to hide gaps is to simply list your years of employment, rather than listing the months. For example, if you worked somewhere from January 2000 – September 2001 and then had a gap from 9/11 until January 2002, you can omit the months and only list the years of employment (2000 – 2001) instead. If you choose to use this format, follow it consistently for all of your work experience. A savvy recruiter will realize that you are trying to cover up a gap and will question you about the specific months once they get you on the phone. The good news is that, at that point, your toe is already in the door, and you can explain the circumstances live, rather than trying to explain them on paper. Be prepared to explain what activities you were involved in during the gap. Volunteering at church or helping to coach a little league team will be seen as positive experiences whereas just sitting home staring at your computer and responding to ads will not.

Many parents have gaps because they took several years off from work to raise their children. Anyone who has ever been a parent knows that this job is THE most difficult one you'll ever have, so instead of thinking of those years as gaps in employment, think of them as a different kind of employment. Consider listing your mommy or daddy related responsibilities in the same section of your resume as your work experiences. Some recruiters will appreciate a title such as "Domestic Engineer" or "Manager of Domestic Affairs" along with a cleverly written but brief job description. A more correct title would be "Organizational Expert, Pep Talker, Chauffeur, Mediator, Chef, & Life Conductor" but I recommend that you save that one for another purpose. You can use your cover letter to explain how you have kept your skills up-to-date while parenting and are completely committed to returning to the workforce.

> ***Absolutely Abby's Advice:*** *Prepare a good reason for any gaps on your resume in addition to an explanation of what activities you were involved in that may have enhanced your career, including personal activities. Gaps are typically not the reason why candidates are rejected. It's the inability to explain them sufficiently, and or a lack of confidence about them that is likely to be a concern for recruiters.*

▪ 17 ▪ Accomplishment Acknowledgements

Do you know how many resumes I receive when I place an ad for a Customer Service Representative? If I am recruiting for a company that practically everyone wants to work for, like Apple or Microsoft, you can probably double the number you chose. So how do I to decide which of the candidates who applied to call? I actually need your help in making my decision – I need you to help me better understand why I should choose you.

Let's first review several of the responsibilities of a Customer Service Representative in a typical call center:

1) Answer incoming phone calls

2) Take orders from customer

3) Enter orders into a computer

4) Handle irate customers

5) Provide customer service

How many of the 1000 resumes that I receive just list bullets, similar to those above, under the title of Customer Service Representative? Usually it's 990. So what do the other 10% do? They are the ones who tell me WHY they are the best Customer Service Representative I could possibly hire. Then they prove their point with a compressive list of accomplishments.

What I want to know about you is not that you know how to answer phones and help customers. I knew that before I even received your resume because that's what a Customer Service Representative does. What I don't know is whether YOU EXCEL at doing these things.

I want to know if you help more customers in less time than your peers. I want to know if you turn 100% of your irate customers into satisfied customers. I want to know if any of your customers called your boss to tell them how wonderful you were. I want to know if you enter the majority of your orders without mistakes. Those are the things I will ask you during your interview, but the way to get the interview in the first place is to make sure that I know about them on paper.

Now, before you go ahead and just add these accomplishments to your resume, take some time to think about how you can prove each of these to your next interviewer. Listing them is a good first step. Take it a bit further by arming yourself with printouts of e-mails from satisfied customers, letters of recommendation from former managers, and/or solid samples of your work (the public work you can share, but not the proprietary materials that are confidential). If you don't have these kinds of documents at your disposal, start collecting them at your next job in case you need them again in the future.

> ***Absolutely Abby's Advice:*** *The competition for jobs has been fierce since the beginning of time. Think of all the things that make you different and special, and write those on your resume. Think of any honors or awards that you've won, even if they are from a while ago as intelligence is never obsolete. Good performance tends to be consistent over time. Tell me on your resume why I should hire YOU, not just what you do every day at your job. Acknowledge your accomplishments and you'll get Absolute applause.*

▪ 18 ▪ An Education on Education

Many candidates struggle with the order in which to place their educational credentials on their resume. There are several rules of the road that seem to apply universally.

If you graduated school more than five years ago, your educational credentials should be listed below your experiences. Work accomplishments become more valuable to a potential employer than education as your career grows. There are three exceptions:

1) If you recently received a new degree, such as an MBA, you may want to list it near the top of your resume to highlight your accomplishments.

2) If you are changing careers and the position you are targeting is more relevant to your degree than it is to your work experience, you may want to list your degree near the top. For example, if you graduated in Accounting, took a customer service position to gain some experience, and are now applying for accounting positions, you should put your education near the top to highlight your credentials.

3) If you have a PhD or a technical degree that you believe will enable you to command a higher salary or title, you may want to put your education before your experience.

If you have taken other training classes, or if you have received certifications in your field, these should Absolutely be listed on your resume. Be careful to spell them correctly as employers will do searches on these keywords.

Once you have several years of relevant work experience, there is no longer a need to list the specific coursework related to your degrees. Earlier in your career, your courses can help employers understand the details of your knowledge when they are trying to place you into an entry-level position.

If you did not graduate college, PLEASE, please, please, do not indicate that you did on your resume. Time and time again, I have seen candidates, who claim to have graduated, be rejected for a job once their background check unveils their deception to the HR department. If you completed some college coursework, you may list it as "Completed 125 credits towards a BA in Manager of Information Systems at California State University." Own up to the reasons why you did not start or finish high school or college – there is typically a good reason behind it and while not every employer understands them, the one who decides to hire you will.

> **Absolutely Abby's Advice:** *Your education is an achievement that you should be proud regardless of whether it is a diploma, an undergraduate degree or a graduate degree. All of those tests you took, those papers you wrote, and those computer programs you tackled put you on the path of progress. Be proud of these accomplishments but also learn to explain why you may have fallen short in certain cases. Keep learning as your career grows and you will find yourself again and again at the head of the class!*

▪ 19 ▪ Making the Grade

When you're positioning a whoopee cushion on your English teacher's chair or passing notes to your best friend in Philosophy, you typically aren't thinking about how your grades are going to affect you when you get to the real world. Does that mean that you have a hurdle to overcome if you were the class clown? Sometimes yes and sometimes no. The importance of your grades to your professional success depends on several factors.

If you are an entry-level candidate, grades do matter. It's that simple. After all, grades are one of the only ways for us to truly evaluate you at this stage of your career. Once you have five or more years of experience under your belt, grades are barely a topic of conversation.

However, specific industries evaluate candidates' grades more than others. In investment banking for example, a low GPA is a ticket to the exit row whereas in sales or customer service, recruiters are much less concerned.

As for the answer to the question about whether to include your GPA on your resume, it really depends on your success. If you graduated Cum Laude or Phi Beta Kappa or if you were elected into the honor society, those achievements should be permanent fixtures on your resume. Success never becomes obsolete. The same goes for a 4.0 GPA. If you are that successful, do not be afraid to tell the world. At the same time, if you did not graduate with a 4.0, you should remove your GPA from your resume after you have three or more years of work experience. And, you should probably not list your GPA if it was below 3.0.

So what if you were the class clown or the note passer, or what if multiple choice tests and essays just weren't your thing? It's simple. Accept who you are and be able to explain it IF it comes up during an interview. In most cases it won't, unless you just graduated.

A low GPA can be due to a variety of factors. Perhaps you had to work 40 hours a week to pay for your tuition. Perhaps you were the leader of a variety of different school clubs, taking time away from your studies. Perhaps you have a learning disability that wasn't identified early enough to help you excel. Perhaps you just weren't ready to apply yourself. Whatever it is, be ready to explain the reason, what you learned from the experience, and how you have risen beyond it to be a stellar performer, regardless.

> ***Absolutely Abby's Advice:*** *If you were a superstar student, do not be afraid to share your success, especially on paper. If not, being able to explain to an interviewer why your grades are not a good indicator of your performance, will be paramount to your success.*

▪ 20 ▪ Being Interesting Counts

People typically hire people they like and/or people that are interesting to them. In 1993 I was the esteemed Long Island Women's Table Tennis Champion.

In 1994 I realized that I was ready to make a career change from sales to Human Resources. I answered approximately twenty recruitment ads and was called by the Human Resources Manager for one of the companies. He said that he decided to call me, despite the fact that I had very little experience, because he wanted to meet the woman who was crowned Table Tennis Champion. True story, I promise. I loved that job and hired 525 technical professionals to jump-start my recruiting career – all because I listed my successful ping-pong tournament on my resume. Go figure!

Now back to you…if you have any hobbies that you think might be even a bit interesting to a recruiter or hiring manager, consider listing them on your resume and on your social media profiles. Avoid listing hobbies such as bug collecting, or cabbage patch doll hairstyling, or frog dissecting, for obvious reasons. Think twice about hobbies that indicate your religious, sports or political affiliations because an unscrupulous hiring manager may move to the next candidate if they have an opposing opinion. Also, avoid putting sentences such as this one in your cover letter, "In my spare time between campaigning for Dan Quayle, I coordinated a trip to see the Yankees for my Catholic Church.

> *Absolutely Abby's Advice:* *Remember, as interesting or as boring as you think you are, someone else always has the opposite opinion. That same person may just end up being your next boss!*

▪ 21 ▪   Take Off Your Mask

In America, Halloween is traditionally a holiday where we don masks and enjoy stepping into the shoes of a character unlike ourselves. Those who are angels in real life can become devils for the day, and those people who are shy or timid can become a superhero.

A resume is similar to a Halloween costume. It's the paper version of you. It's your mask. But, unlike a Halloween costume, a resume must be the real version of you, not a version of you that you wish you could be. Your accomplishments on your resume should be front and center so that no one can miss them. It should be a document that you are proud of when you read it. Because your resume is your "personal marketing collateral", it needs to be the "best you" that it can be, without going beyond the truth. It should be nonfiction and written with a marketing spin, to make you look like the most attractive candidate to the reader.

During interviews, it's relatively easy to put on a mask. When someone asks how well you know Microsoft Word, it's simple to say that you are an expert when the job calls for an expert. It's simple, but is it right?

Obviously the answer is no, but it's for a different reason than you might think. If you use your mask to influence a company to hire you, when you're secretly not really qualified and/or secretly not passionate about the job, nobody wins. So if the job calls for a Microsoft Word expert and you aren't one, consider an honest answer such as "I would not necessarily consider myself an expert, but I quickly teach myself new features as I need them." Your honesty might save you from ending up in a job you can't handle. Better yet, you might have better odds of landing the job if the hiring manager appreciates your integrity.

When Halloween ends, off comes your mask, much like the first few weeks in your new job. If you oversold yourself, you will soon be discovered when your new boss asks you to take on a new project. How will you feel if you claimed that you had a certain expertise but now don't have the ability to complete the project? How will your boss feel about you?

> **Absolutely Abby's Advice:** *For a moment, glance at your resume, and then take a long hard look at yourself in the mirror. Is your resume the image of your best self or is it a façade? During your interviews, are you feigning interest just to get an offer, or do you really love the job? Make every attempt to be honest with both yourself and your new employer so that you end up in the right place at the right time. Let's all take off our masks together!*

▪ 22 ▪   Cover Letter Conquests

Remember the last time you went shopping for a big-ticket item such as a car? The salesman showed you a shiny, professional piece of collateral that explained the car in great detail. Could you have learned about the car without the collateral? Of course! But the collateral is part of the sales pitch – it explains the features and benefits of the car and tells you why you should buy it.

Your cover letter is your resume's collateral, and its purpose is to highlight your strengths to the reader. I continue to hear stories about jobseekers who were far less qualified than their competition and landed in positions anyway. In almost every case, the jobseekers wrote a stellar cover letter to get their foot in the door, so by the time they arrived to the interview, they were already way ahead of their competition.

You should include a cover letter as often as possible, but at least when you are applying for a job that you are extremely interested in. Consider asking a marketing friend to critique your letter to ensure that it is marketing you in the best way possible.

Make an attempt to address your letter to an actual person, rather than just using Dear Sir or Madam. To find the name of the hiring manager, use Google or LinkedIn. Even a good guess scores you points, because it indicates that you tried harder than everyone else.

Make sure that you mention the name of the company in the letter, followed by an explanation of why you are interested in working for THIS company in particular. Make sure that you really mean what you say. Recruiters have a way of sensing when you are being less than truthful. Our goal is to hire people who *sincerely* want to work for our company – it's the job of your cover letter to convince us.

At the same time as you are writing creatively, proofread your letter to be sure that your writing is grammatically correct. When recruiters are faced with large stacks of resumes for certain positions, you will not make the first cut if they discover spelling or grammar mistakes on your resume or cover letter. These mistakes are the eye's equivalent of "nails on a chalkboard".

Over the years, I've saved a dozen or so resumes that had comical mistakes on them. I refer to these affectionately as my "Wall of Shame".

Here are just a few examples from cover letters that ended up in my collection:

1) A fast-paced company is not the same thing as a "face paced", a "fast paised", or even a "fast paste" company. Perhaps someone who uses the keyboard shortcut CTRL+V believes that they are working at a "fast paste" speed. I think not.

2) The abbreviation for Assistant is Asst. Please don't ever forget that. When you drop the "t" from "Asst" you aren't offering much to be proud of.

3) Hiring is not the same thing as "highering" or "hiering" or "hireing"

Double check, triple check and quadruple check your cover letter. And then check it again. You can never be too obsessed about getting the details right.

> ***Absolutely Abby's Advice:*** *Your cover letter is your sales presentation and it can make you or break you. The key is to give the reader a small glimpse into your background, which encourages them to want to learn more by reading your resume. As simple as this sounds, writing a good cover letter takes practice and patience. Trust me…it will be Absolutely worth all the hard work if you get it right.*

▪ 23 ▪ The Posting Puzzle

As with so many job search related questions, there is no one right answer. Everyone you meet may have a slightly different opinion about which boards to try, which ads to respond to, which headhunters to work with, and which social media networks to join. The thing to do is to take in all the opinions, and then make a decision about which feels right for you.

The most important thing you can do is to let everyone know that you are searching and what you are specifically searching for. So, do I think you should post your resume online? Absolutely and positively YES. Despite the increase in the number of recruiters searching on social media sites and in their own resume databases, a significant number are still searching the major boards, so your resume needs to be posted there in order for you to be discovered.

Now, should you post your resume on every job site out there? Absolutely NO! It's just not the best use of your time. Post your resume on one or two of the main boards and then, search for niche sites related to your industry or profession, and post on some of the most popular ones. And, consider posting your resume on the company career portals of the leaders in your industry, because many corporate recruiters search their databases first before looking externally.

While I believe this advice serves the large majority of jobseekers, you may meet headhunters who recommend against your posting online, because they will be unable to present you to certain companies who will be able to also find you on a job board for free. If you plan to search with the help of a headhunter, you may want to contact a few first to see which companies they are working with before starting to post online.

> *Absolutely Abby's Advice:* *Take charge of your job search and do what is best for you, both personally and professionally. Have a presence on the most effective job boards for your profession and also on online networking sites such as LinkedIn. By getting your information out into the "jobosphere", you are much more likely to be found by the recruiters who are searching for you.*

▪ 24 ▪ Job Boards In Contention for Your Attention

These days there are a variety of job posting sites, some of which require a small investment. The question is whether or not they are worth the expense. The following are, what I would consider, the top job search sites in contention for your attention.

The Oldies But Goodies: Monster, CareerBuilder & Hotjobs

First and foremost, I recommend that you post your resume on all three of these sites because you can't be sure which companies are searching on which boards. Hiding your name or e-mail address will often discourage recruiters from attempting to contact you, so I recommend against it. If you are concerned that your current employer will find your resume online if they are sniffing around for current employees, simply change the name of your current company to "Confidential Company". On all job boards that you post your resume on, I would avoid posting your salary so that you are not screened out by the job board's search functionality prematurely. To save time, set up "job search agents" on all three boards so that you receive daily e-mails of new jobs that match your preferences.

The Blasters: ResumeRabbit, ResumeViper & ResumeZapper

Besides these three sites, there are probably ten others. They all do approximately the same thing – they blast your resume to hiring managers and recruiters. The problem is this – if recruiters don't click on your resume and open it, it doesn't matter whether or not it is in their mailbox.

Even if your resume is opened, it does not include a personalized cover letter and is not targeted for a specific job. Therefore, my recommendation is that you use these services only if they are free or if nothing else seems to be working. Before signing up with a particular resume blaster, determine whether employers need to opt in to their service or whether they just receive resumes without asking. There is a major distinction.

The Six Figure Experts: The Ladders, ExecuNet & SixFigureJobs

Over the years, I have heard mixed reviews about these sites for 100K+ jobseekers. Some people swear by them and others say that the positions on these boards are similar to positions they find elsewhere. Since SixFigureJobs is free, I'd search there for jobs and also set up a profile. For the other two, which you have to invest in, I'd suggest paying for one month only and then determining if they are worth continuing for future months.

The Diversity Sites: DiversityInc, DiversityWorking & MinorityJobs

If you are a jobseeker and you consider yourself to be a diversity candidate, I highly recommend sharing that information with the world. Most larger organizations these days have diversity programs and are trying to attract candidates to their sites. They are using specific boards to find you so you should post your resume on at least a few on these sites. And when you post your resume on Monster, be sure to check off that you are a diversity candidate so that you are included in Monster's diversity database, which is sold to recruiters separately.

The Niche Sites: Dice, HigherEdJobs, HealthECareers, Medzilla, Biospace, MediaBistro, JobsInTheMoney, CareerBank, LawJobs, etc.

Every profession has a host of niche boards that are specific to their industry. Whether you should post your resume or profile on all of the relevant niche boards is questionable, but you should definitely be searching on all of them weekly, if not daily.

<u>The Aggregators: Indeed, SimplyHired & JobCircle</u>

The aggregators do an excellent job of searching the web to find positions that match the criteria that you enter. They search all of the sites listed above in addition to thousands of other websites, including company job portals. You should definitely set up a daily search agent on all three sites, and you may find that these actually turn out to be your best leads. The one downside to all three aggregators is that their search functionality is extremely basic. You are limited to searching by keyword and zip code only, so you may receive leads that are completely irrelevant, accidentally. When their search functionality improves, the aggregators will be a force to be reckoned with.

> ***Absolutely Abby's Advice:*** *When you are operating in a competitive job market, less is not more…instead, more is more. You have to work a little bit harder, be a little stronger than everyone else, and get to hiring managers a little bit faster. Unless you have ESP, you don't know what exact thing that you do, or what site that you post on, is going to be the ultimate ticket to your success. So, keep digging and keep at it. Eventually, your number will be up and you will hit the jackpot!*

▪ 25 ▪ The Social Media Trio

Unless you've been hiding under a rock, you've probably noticed that networking and social media are the "in" things right now.

So why are recruiters investing their time and energy in tools like LinkedIn, Twitter, and Facebook instead of just searching for candidates on the job boards? (At this point you should be gleefully humming your favorite game show theme to get the full effect of my question).

The answer is…they are FREE. FREE for you and FREE for companies. There are ways to pay a little more to get a little more functionality on both sides, but the basic level is currently FREE. With companies in almost every industry trimming their recruiting budgets, there is nothing better than a FREE tool. Have I mentioned that the "Social Media Trio" are FREE?

Traditionally, tools such as Monster, CareerBuilder, and Hotjobs have always been free for you, whereas recruiters have spent big bucks to use them. According to a survey by Jobvite, a recruiting software provider, as companies cut costs, the social networking sites have become excellent sourcing tools. Of the 440 HR professionals surveyed, 72% said their company will invest more in recruiting through social media in the coming years. Meanwhile, more than half expect to spend less on job boards. That is not to say that recruiters don't still use Monster & CareerBuilder as well, but social media has thrown its hat in the ring and is here to stay.

The Jobvite survey indicated that LinkedIn is used by 80% of those who responded, Twitter is used by 42% and Facebook is used by 36%. We are seeing rapid growth in social media use and will continue to see it as time goes on. So does this mean that you're missing the boat if you're only using the job boards? Absolutely!

Here's how recruiters are using the Social Media Trio:

1) LinkedIn – Recruiters join LinkedIn groups to search for candidates from particular industries or professions. They also search directly through their LinkedIn network. The great thing about LinkedIn is that you can not only search for the people who you are directly connected to, but you can also search for the people who know the people that you are connected to. This way, with at least 100 connections of your own, you can be a part of a

much larger network. So, a recruiter doesn't need to be directly connected to you to be able to find you.

2) Facebook – Recruiters create Facebook Pages and Facebook Groups and then post their jobs in there. They also search in Groups and on Pages where similar people gather to have intelligent career-related conversations. And…many of them will accept your "friend" request so that you can see the jobs they have open as an updated status on their profile. Remember to be careful of what you post on these kinds of sites. Avoid posting embarrassing pictures and snippets of crude language or grammatically incorrect language. Also avoid bashing current or former employers and negative comments. Remember that these sites are searchable and will remain so for a long time.

3) Twitter – With Twitter, you simply "follow" all of the headhunters in your industry and read their daily tweets about the jobs they are working on. You can also start up intelligent conversations with people in your profession or industry. Note the word "intelligent" again. While Twitter started with people telling each other that they were going to the fridge for a glass of milk, it has now evolved into a useful tool for jobseekers and recruiters alike. Recruiters are searching profiles to find candidates as we speak so start tweeting! Again, it's free and it's easy!

So am I telling you to stop using Monster & CareerBuilder? Quite the contrary! Many organizations continue to use these sites, so you need to be active there as well. These sites offer you the opportunity to post a full resume and choose your detailed work-related preferences, whereas LinkedIn, Facebook, and Twitter are less robust when it comes to job search profiles. And, don't just search on these sites – post your resume so that you can be found by people that you didn't know were hunting for you (that's why they call them headhunters).

Imagine you are a recruiter searching for yourself. Where would you search for you? What sites would you look at? What networking groups would you join? Finding yourself is more than half the battle.

> **Absolutely Abby's Advice:** *You can use an oven to cook with rather than a microwave, but your competition will nuke you as you wait for your job search to reach 400 degrees. To increase your chances of being found, jump on board the social media plane, strap on your seat belt, and soar to success!*

▪ 26 ▪ Picture Perfect

A frequent question that jobseekers ask me is whether to post their picture online on their LinkedIn, Facebook, or Twitter profile. Social media is just that – it's a way to be social and to build your network. One major necessity of being social is getting to know someone, and in my opinion, there's no better way to get to know someone than to see what he or she looks like. Even some phones now have the ability for you to see the person who you are speaking with.

A picture makes your profile seem more personal, and makes you appear to be approachable. Being approachable is the first step towards building a strong relationship and therefore, a strong network. After all, how can you develop relationships without encouraging people to approach you?

Another reason to put a picture on your profile is this: recruiters will be suspicious if you don't, the same way they are suspicious about resumes that don't include years or months.

If you choose to include a picture, remember that a picture is only worth a thousand words if it is professional looking and photogenic. Ideally, have a headshot taken by a professional photographer. If you are on a tighter budget, consider having your picture taken at Sears or Wal*Mart for a small fee. As a last resort, have a friend take a picture of you with a digital camera, but not with a camera phone. Select a neutral background outside to stand in front of on a cloudy day or in indirect sunlight.

Ensure that any picture posted on your social media sites is professional. When you are searching for a job, your picture should be of you, not a picture of your family or your dog. Avoid posting pictures of you dressed up like SpongeBob on Halloween drinking a martini. Make sure the pictures you post present you as a person worthy of hiring. Your attitude in your picture should exude confidence. After all, if you believe you are a superstar, everyone should know that at first glance. Your picture should also be timely. It should be a good representation of who you are today.

If you decide to put a picture of yourself on your resume, it MUST be a professional photo. Pictures on resumes are more common outside the United States. The pictures should be used to show your professionalism, not your attractiveness. There is a HUGE difference.

Pictures on business cards are also starting to become more popular. I actually like the idea because with all the cards I acquire, it's nice to be able to attach a face to each name. Remember that the card will be passed among many other people, so it is critical that you look your best. You should avoid printing them at home on inkjet paper because the ink runs when it gets wet.

Now, let's discuss the elephant in the room... discrimination. Many people don't want to post their pictures online because they fear that recruiters will pre-judge them based on their age, race, ethnicity, weight, etc. A friend of mine who is a career coach had a good answer to this. He said, "why would you want to interview with someone in the first place who won't hire you because of how you look?" He's right. If someone is going to discriminate against you, it's better to know before you waste your time with him or her. In my opinion, the benefits of showing the world who you are far outweigh the risks. You are who you are. No one can change that. Only if you believe in yourself first will the world join you.

> ***Absolutely Abby's Advice:*** *Picture this… you add your photo to your LinkedIn profile today. Everyone you are connected with gets a message saying that you updated your profile. One of those people happens to take a look at your photo and he thinks, "wow…what a friendly looking Tech Support Rep that is." Then, he realizes that his company is hiring Tech Support Reps and he remembers about the referral bonus he will get paid if he introduces you. Bing bang boom… you have an interview. Pay for the professional photo… it's worth every cent!*

▪ 27 ▪   Are you a LION?

LinkedIn is a trusted online network of more than 53 million experienced professionals from over 200 countries representing 170 industries. After signing up for LinkedIn, you create a profile that summarizes your professional expertise and accomplishments. You can then form networking connections by inviting your contacts to join LinkedIn and connect to you. Your network consists of your connections, your connections' connections, and the people they know, linking you to a vast number of qualified professionals. Your professional network of trusted contacts is one of your most valuable assets. Through your network, you can discover inside connections that can help you with your job search.

Similar to a resume, your LinkedIn profile is where you tell the world all about yourself, but as usual, you have choices to make. Here are some questions to consider as you are setting up your profile:

Are you interesting?

The answer to this is that you're as interesting as your profile is. If you do any volunteer work or participate in extra-curricular activities, consider adding them to your profile (and to your resume). You never know who might read your profile and want to learn more about you. Only post activities that indicate your professionalism, similar to those that are on your resume.

Are you Honest Abe?

These days, almost every recruiter is well connected on LinkedIn, which means that they use it frequently to find candidates. In a survey conducted by the Electronic Recruiter's Exchange (ERE.com), 64% of the recruiters reported that they use LinkedIn to do background research. That means that your dates of employment, dates of graduation, and job titles listed on your profile MUST match your resume exactly.

Are you reachable?

Whether or not to list your e-mail address on your profile is a decision you should not take lightly. When you are conducting a job search, it is important that people who want to contact you can do so with ease, whether they find you on LinkedIn or on a job board. There are many reasons why people choose to keep their e-mail addresses on LinkedIn confidential. However, if you don't list your e-mail on your profile, a recruiter has to rely on someone that is connected to you to make the introduction. If your e-mail is listed on your profile, you remove the middleman.

Are you a LION?

Frequently you will see the term LION on a profile, which stands for LinkedIn Open Networker. A LION is someone who agrees to accept LinkedIn invitations from anyone who sends them, regardless of whether they know them personally. The people who designate themselves as LIONS are typically business owners, headhunters, and people who love to connect other people together. While you are a jobseeker, you may wish to become an open networker, simply to increase the number of connections you have to people that can help you. As a LION myself, I invite you to connect to me as well.

> ***Absolutely Abby's Advice:*** *LinkedIn is a powerful networking tool that will help you get a few steps closer to your ideal job. Take the time to develop an effective LinkedIn profile and you will have added another powerful way for recruiters to find you.*

▪ 28 ▪ Building Your LinkedIn Network

Joining LinkedIn and creating a detailed profile is the first step towards developing a professional network online. Knowing how to grow your network is the next essential piece of the puzzle. Once you're signed up, you build your network by connecting with people you've known for a while, people you recently met, and some people that you would like to meet.

The easiest way to add someone to your network is to send them a request to connect with you by clicking on "Add X to your network." Of course, this requires that you already know their e-mail address. Thus the best place to get started building your network is with the people you already know.

You can also take some time each week to review the lists of former classmates and co-workers that appear on your home page. Thanks to LinkedIn, if you know any of the people on the lists, you can send them a request to connect without even knowing their e-mail address.

Next, add people who you meet at live networking events. When you exchange business cards with a new person, mention that you use LinkedIn to keep track of your networking connections and ask if they mind if you send them an invitation. This gesture will make them far more likely to welcome your outreach and accept your invitation when they receive it.

A good way to find people to connect with, who have similar interests, is to join several groups that relate to the type of work you've done and the type of work you'd consider doing. For example, if you are a scientist, you may want to join a biotech or pharmaceutical LinkedIn Group. If you are a nurse, you may want to join a group for a specific hospital in your area or a group that discusses healthcare issues. Once you join a group, you can send out requests for introductions to other members without knowing their e-mail addresses.

Make sure that you also join any relevant job seeking groups in your industry. For example, if you are an IT Technician on LinkedIn, join the "IT Specialist" Group. If you are in Human Resources, join the Society of Human Resources Management (SHRM) Group. If you are in the pharmaceutical industry, join the "Pharmaceutical Professionals Worldwide Network" Group. Why should you join these kinds of groups? Because recruiters use the groups as a starting point when searching for candidates.

One way to gain recognition on LinkedIn and also attract more connections is to provide answers to questions that other people ask. Simply click on the "Answers" tab on the top of the page to get to the Q&A section. Then, search for questions that you can offer expert opinions on and type away! When answering the questions, consider including a note to readers that says, "Please connect with me on LinkedIn" with your e-mail address included. To attract more attention to your profile, consider asking intelligent industry-related questions that will elicit responses from like-minded people. You never know whether one of them is looking to fill a position tailor-made for you.

As an added bonus, you can also build your network with the LIONs or "Linked In Open Networkers". You can find them by searching on

LinkedIn by typing "LION" in the keyword search field. Then, just send them an invitation, which they will happily accept.

Once you have 50-100 networking connections, you can ask your connections to introduce you to hiring managers and recruiters by clicking on "Get introduced though a connection." That is the power of LinkedIn.

> **Absolutely Abby's Advice:** *LinkedIn becomes an extremely valuable job search tool, once your network is at least 50-100 people in size. To grow your network, use the technology built into the LinkedIn platform by joining groups, answering questions and searching for former friends and colleagues that you have lost touch with. As always, the best way to grow your network is to develop it in person at face-to-face networking events. Then, LinkedIn becomes the perfect vehicle to help keep your information about your connections up-to-date.*

▪ 29 ▪ Joining the Blogosphere

My thoughts about becoming a blogger to get noticed by recruiters and prospective companies are similar to my opinions regarding social media. Using these tools in the right way can be extremely effective for a job search, but using them incorrectly can spell disaster. Here are five considerations:

Your blog theme should be relevant

If your recent job experience is in finance and you are currently searching for a similar role, blogging about the industry can be a terrific way to showcase your talents. Blogging about an industry that you are attempting to get into is a wonderful way to unveil your expertise to the professionals you'd like to meet. It also proves that you already speak the industry language. Lastly, blogging about your search in general can also be appropriate – just maintain a positive attitude throughout your journey.

Your blog topics should be non-controversial

Avoid blogging about topics where people typically take sides. You don't want your interviewers to disagree with you before they get a chance to meet you. For example, blogging about your political views or your religious views should be avoided. Blogging about a sports team can also be tricky as there are many famous rivalries and personal biases that may get in your way of success. These same controversial topics should be avoided during an interview for the same reasons.

Your blogs should be non-confrontational

Whatever you choose to write about, be sure that you are writing with a positive tone. You want to avoid being seen as derogatory, condescending, arrogant, hostile, and/or bitter. Almost everything you post on-line is searchable by employers – so don't post anything you wouldn't want your next interviewer, your spouse, your parents, or your current boss to read about you.

Your blogs should be professional looking

Choose a blog template or theme that suits your personality, but also be sure that it is professionally designed. Many bloggers use WordPress to set up their blogs because it is user friendly. WordPress offers thousands of professional looking templates as well so be sure that your blog will be visually appealing to your audience. Consider bartering with a web designer or asking a friend to get you started if you struggle technically or artistically.

Your blogs should be professionally written

As with resumes and cover letters, grammar and spelling count when you are blogging. If a potential employer finds your blog, you can be sure they will be evaluating your writing skills. If you don't have access to a professional editor, consider partnering with another blogger or a friend who can edit your posts. You may have a stellar cover letter and resume, but if your blog shows the truth about your writing skills, the game will be over.

> *Absolutely Abby's Advice: When you are a blogger, the world is your stage. Like any skill you wish to perfect, blogging takes some practice, but it can be a wonderful way to express your thoughts and feelings, while also adding value to the lives of others. Visit StartingABlog.com for tips on how to get started. Once you are ready to commit to regular posts, choose a professional template and then launch yourself into the blogosphere. I look forward to meeting you there!*

▪ 30 ▪ Increasing Your Shares

In 2005, I was introduced to three wonderful in-transition groups in the New York City metropolitan area. Each month I would attend the meeting to garner advice on how to network, how to create a spectacular cover letter, and how to write the perfect resume. Some of my favorite relationships came from those groups and still remain strong today.

Attending the groups wasn't the whole story. Each networking group also had set up an online Yahoo group where members could share job leads. Day after day and week after week, a few leads would be sent in by our members, with the rest coming from our fearless leaders who collected them from around town.

Sharing is something we learn how to do as a young child. We share our ice cream, we share our toys, and we share things we learn. Sharing helps us grow and enables us to make a difference in other people's lives. Think of the last time that you shared some knowledge with someone that helped change his or her life.

It's really very simple. The more you pay it forward and share information, the more that your fellow jobseekers will do the same. You can't network if you can't share. You have to be able to help someone first before they will have any desire to help you. That's what "paying it forward" is all about.

The next time you receive a job lead that you are not interested in or qualified for, don't just hit delete. Think of all the possible places you can post it...think of all the possible people that would benefit by seeing it. Think of your Facebook groups, your LinkedIn groups, your Yahoo groups, and your in-transition groups. If everyone sent in one lead a week to their respective groups, each person in the group would have access to 500-1000 leads per week which would be tremendous for recruiters and candidates alike! Together, we could be making a huge difference.

The kinds of leads that are worth sharing are the ones that not everyone knows about. Going onto Monster and sending out leads that the general population has access to gives you an A for effort, but is not the most effective way of "paying it forward". What's worth sharing are the "underground job leads", the ones that are hidden from the average jobseeker's radar. For example, share information about positions that recruiters call you about that you are not interested in applying for. Share the leads that you receive via e-mail or on LinkedIn that you have no interest in. Share positions that you find out about from a friend, a networking buddy, or another in-transition group.

When you start sharing leads, suddenly everyone will know who you are. You will become an instant hero as you start to share yourself and your knowledge with the world. And then, keep your eyes on your inbox as more leads suddenly start pouring in as a result of your generosity.

> *Absolutely Abby's Advice: Imagine how it would feel tomorrow morning if you woke up and found the lead for your perfect job in your e-mail. Then, imagine landing the job. How grateful would you be that someone sent that lead in for you? How much would you want to run over to that person's house and give them a great big hug? Now think what it would be like if you were the person being hugged. What if you shared a lead that wasn't right for you but it was perfect for someone else? It's a wonderful feeling to help someone else. Just imagine how you will feel the day that someone calls you to thank you for the lead that you posted that ultimately became his or her next job. Perhaps one day, you'll be the one doing the thanking.*

▪ 31 ▪ Paying Attention to Your Application

You may remember the days when you would sit in the waiting area where a receptionist watched over you silently as you nervously tried to decide what information to enter on your job application. Nowadays, online job applications are just as common as cell phones, and they are becoming even more widespread as Human Resources departments move farther and farther away from paper-based processing. Any day now, I'm expecting to see a company accepting applications via text message.

When it comes to online applications, here are several things to remember:

1) Job codes – If you are applying for a specific position, make sure that you enter the correct job code as this helps the applicant tracking system put you in the correct bucket. If you use the wrong ones, your resume may kick the bucket or never be found in the haystack.

2) Salary information – Avoid entering your compensation if it is not a requirement. As much as I, the recruiter, want you to enter the information, I, Absolutely Abby, recommend against it. If I,

the recruiter, know your salary range before you know the job's salary range I, the recruiter, have the upper hand in the negotiation.

3) Cover letter – If the application asks for a cover letter, you should definitely insert one. Make sure that your grammar is in tip-top shape and that your letter demonstrates your creativity. Every word you use from now until you are hired is being evaluated.

4) Spelling – If there are free form fields in the application where you have to enter in school names or former company names, be sure that you spell them correctly. This is not just because spelling errors are a cause for concern to a recruiter, but also because a misspelled word means a missed keyword matching opportunity.

5) Follow directions – If the application instructs you to fill a field out in a certain way, make sure that you do it. If you can't follow instructions on an application, how will you be able to follow instructions on the job? Or, will you disrespect authority once hired? This will be in the mind of the recruiter reviewing your application.

> *Absolutely Abby's Advice: As simple a task as filling out an online application appears, you need to make sure that you spend the necessary time to fill it out completely and correctly. An application is a legal employment document, so it is Absolutely critical that you answer it honestly so that down the road there is no cause for concern.*

▪ 32 ▪ Social Insecurity & Your Birthday

Jobseekers frequently ask me how much to reveal to employers at an early stage of the process. More specifically, the question is whether you should provide your date of birth and social security number to a potential employer for a background check before you receive an offer of employment. The answer depends on the employer and the recruiter.

The answer is really very straightforward. Simply ask if you can provide your social security number and date of birth later in the process. In some cases, the answer will be a flat out no, especially when you are asking a computer screen, not a person. But if in fact you are filling out a paper application, ask the recruiter if you can save that information until the time that they actually need to use it.

The question though is when they truly need to have it. They usually need to have it when they run your background check, but typically not before. However, some companies use your social security number to enter you into their database and track you as an applicant, in which case they may not consider you an applicant without having that number. And some companies run your background check long before you receive an offer.

If you are applying online to an ad and are required to fill out this information online before you have spoken with a live person at the company, you will probably have more difficulty getting around this issue. In many cases, the computer will not let you get past the first page without answering the social security question. If you are extremely reluctant to provide it, you can try to enter 000-00-0000 and see if the system barks back at you. But, entering an invalid social security number is not exactly following directions, so I personally would not make that choice. If you do decide to enter your social security number, just make sure that the website is a) an actual company's application, and b) an "https" site rather than "http" and c) a company that you really want to work for enough to give them your social security number.

If a company does ask for this personal information early in the process, they typically include a statement on why they need it, and the statement usually confirms that they will not use it other than for that specific reason. In most cases, you can rely on that fact. Most employers are honest and are not collecting the information for the wrong reasons.

> ***Absolutely Abby's Advice:*** *My advice on providing social security numbers, birthdates, references, and past salaries is simple. If it is required for you to be an applicant, and you actually want to be an applicant, do not argue with the recruiter or the computer, as it may become your downfall. Asking if you can provide the information down the road is always an option. Just be ready to happily concede if the answer is no.*

▪ 33 ▪ Slicing Up Your Day

When you are unemployed, you should NOT spend every waking moment on your job search. If this surprises you, read on…

In life, doing something to the extreme typically provides a less than stellar result. Going to Atlantic City or Las Vegas every once in a while can be fun for some people, but weekly trips may drill a hole in your wallet. Eating ice cream on a hot summer day is delightful, but eating too much of it causes a tummy-ache. Similarly, spending too much time on certain components of your job search can twist your life out of balance. Here is my suggested breakdown:

<u>Searching & Networking Online – 30% of your time</u>

This 30% includes searching for jobs and posting your resume on the main job boards, niche sites, and company sites. This also includes spending time on social media sites such as LinkedIn, Facebook & Twitter and also networking in Yahoo and Google Groups. Last but not least, it includes time spent searching online for and networking with headhunters.

<u>Live Networking – 30% of your time</u>

Some experts have suggested that approximately two-thirds of people who land in new jobs found their opportunity due to social networking. Attending seminars and in-transition groups and conducting informational interviews are all vital components of networking to be considered. Any activities that help you develop relationships with people, who can introduce you to other people, should become a significant percentage of your weekly routine.

Volunteering – 20% of your time

You may be surprised that this number is so high. To me, volunteering does not mean that you have to work for a non-profit organization. Volunteering is simply the act of reaching out and helping others. You might help other jobseekers with their resume. You might help your friend paint their new apartment. You might help a professional organization run an event. And yes, you might actually volunteer for a hospital, the Red Cross, or Habitat for Humanity. Trust me. Helping others can result in unexpected surprises that may be far beyond your wildest dreams.

Personal Time – 20% of your time

Similar to when you are employed, you should aim for a work/life balance that you are comfortable with, while you are searching for a job. Spend time focusing on improving your health – join a gym, take a yoga class, or start walking around your neighborhood. Spend time with family and friends that you would not normally have, and lean on them for support. Read a book a week – it will give you intelligent things to discuss during your interview. If you feel uncomfortable with 20%, at least consider devoting 10% of your time to yourself. You will soon see how invigorating it can be. And while I haven't studied it in clinical trials, I can say anecdotally that happy and balanced people present better during interviews.

__Absolutely Abby's Advice:__ Spending 100% of your time applying for jobs online is not the best course of action. To meet the right people, you'll need to get out of the house, leap outside your box, and try on some new hats for size. Ultimately, it's up to you how much time you spend on each of these activities – you should always do what feels right for you. But…always, always, always…make sure you give 100% effort to each activity as it's happening.

▪ 34 ▪ Headhunting the Headhunters

One of the most common questions I receive about search firms is "How do I find a headhunter when they aren't already hunting me?" The answer, as usual, depends on your persistence, your motivation, and your creativity, which also happen to be the same three skills that you need in the job market to land quickly.

The best directory of search firms in the United States is the "Directory of Executive Recruiters". Commonly known as "The Red Book", the Directory lists all of the search firms and offers great detail on what they specialize in, where they are located, and how long they have been in business. If you are on a budget, you may wish to look for the book in your library or split the cost with a job search buddy.

On the web, you can search for headhunters on NPAWorldwide.com Many larger search firms also have their own websites where you can find information about what they specialize in. The problem is that you may have trouble finding specific websites because headhunters don't necessarily want to be found. Try searching "engineering headhunter" or "medical device search firm". You'll find some but you will not find many.

Most corporate recruiters and headhunters are using LinkedIn to source candidates, so you should be able to find a profile for them as well. Better yet, you'll find out where they worked before they joined their company, how long they have been in the recruiting industry, and what they specialize in. Best of all, you'll get to read their recommendations from both clients and jobseekers if they have any. The best ones will have several recommendations and will have been headhunting in your industry or occupation for at least 10 years.

There are also LinkedIn Groups and Facebook Pages and Groups where great networking abounds. The most well networked headhunters will be lurking in all of these places and so should you.

> ***Absolutely Abby's Advice:*** *We call them headhunters because that is what they do…they hunt. Most of them would rather hunt than be hunted so you have to think like a headhunter to track them down. If you were a headhunter, what groups would you join? What keywords would you use to advertise your site with? Where would your favorite haunts be? Then, act like a headhunter and go hunting for the hunters.*

▪ 35 ▪ Globetrotting

In some cases, you may be willing to search for and ultimately accept positions outside of your country. Identifying jobs in other parts of the world may appear to be more challenging, but the same job search techniques apply:

Find the international headhunters

Trying to find a job can be a daunting task in itself, but trying to find one outside your state or country adds additional complexities. In many cases, hiring a headhunter with experience in a specific geographical area may be your best bet. To find an international headhunter, simply search on LinkedIn or on www.NPAWorldwide.com in the same way that you would search for a headhunter in your city or state. You may also want to join Xing.com, a global professional networking site similar to LinkedIn.

Search on the job boards

Although Monster, CareerBuilder, and Hotjobs may be effective job search tools in the United States, they may not be as effective in countries like Japan, Italy or India. So how then do you find the best job boards to search on? Simply search for someone in your LinkedIn network who lives in your country of choice and who is working in your industry, and ask for his or her opinions on the subject. You can also join Yahoo Groups or LinkedIn Groups that attract people from the specific country or you can ask a question on LinkedIn to gain the opinions from people in the specific countries or cities you are interested in.

<u>Navigate the corporate maze</u>

One way to get the opportunity to go overseas is via a transfer from your current employer. Search for jobs in companies that have locations outside your country. During your interviews, ask tactful questions about how you might obtain one of those opportunities down the road. For example, ask "What international growth opportunities are available for employees?"

<u>Networking, networking and more networking</u>

A friend of mine who recently moved to China found his job lead because he attended a networking event. He attended the event and then saw the job posted by a recruiter who was a member of the same group. They connected, he interviewed, and within a few months, he was on his way to China. Was this luck? No, my friends, it's just good old fashion networking!

> ***Absolutely Abby's Advice:*** *The moral of the story is this; seek and you shall find! You may need to dig a bit deeper for a position outside of your neighborhood, but if that is your passion, go for it! If you are thinking outside the country, also think outside the box as you search. One day soon you will earn your golden globe.*

▪ 36 ▪ Dedication to Education

As a jobseeker, you may discover skills or certifications that are frequently listed as requirements for positions you are interested in, that you do not currently have. There are many reasons to return to school to further your education while you are searching for a job. Here are some of them:

1) Furthering your education in your field, on your own time, indicates to employers that you take pride in excelling at what you do. Who would not want to hire someone who is dedicated to achievement?

2) The students in your classes will naturally become a part of your network. Perhaps they may even lead you to your new job, but if nothing else, they can become important resources for career success once you land.

3) Going to classes will provide you with some structure during your weekday. It also provides a better answer to the question about what you did while you were out of work than "I just searched for a job."

4) When you have a full-time job, you won't have as much time to take classes, do homework, and write term papers as you have now. There is no time like the present.

5) Best of all, having additional skills and certifications makes you eligible for more positions than you were before.

A jobseeker once asked me if he should go back to school to make him more marketable for management positions that he hadn't been successful at landing in the past. It would seem that the obvious answer to this question should be yes, until you dissect the question further. The answer I gave him on the surface was that I wasn't sure that it necessarily would.

If you have not been able to achieve the salary level or title that you feel you deserve, the reasons may not be so straightforward. You may be lacking in education, job consistency, industry knowledge, leadership skills or aptitude, intrinsic motivation, positive attitude, or something completely different. Rather than trying to determine which of these has held you back on your own, I recommend that you ask your former managers for their honest opinions. But then, be ready to hear them.

Then again, not everyone has to be a manager to be successful. You can be a highly compensated consultant or specialist and still earn a terrific living. So listen carefully to the answers, integrate and embrace the feedback, and then consider how you might gain the tools that are missing from your toolbox, perhaps by taking some additional classes.

> **Absolutely Abby's Advice:** *Additional education will always help your career, but not necessarily in the direct way you expect it to. Heed the lessons you learn as you dig deep and ask the important questions of your mentors, friends and managers. The answers have the power to enlighten you and ultimately help you make dramatic shifts in your career.*

• 37 • Voluntary Volunteering

According to Wikipedia, volunteering is the practice of people working on behalf of others, without being motivated by financial or material gain. Volunteering is an altruistic activity, intended to promote good or improve human quality of life. Aside from the goose bumps that you get when you help the lives of other people, there are also many other added benefits.

Volunteering helps you build your network

Many people who volunteer are currently employers and many are business owners. One of them might just want to hire you based on the passion they witness as you participate in an activity that you are really enjoying.

You just might want to hang your hat there for a while

I volunteered to become the New York City Networking Leader for Whine & Dine, a Human Resources networking group. This position was extremely rewarding because not only did I meet terrific people, but I was also able to teach them the power of networking. What once was a volunteer job, eventually turned into a business opportunity that I still enjoy today.

You can list your volunteer jobs as experiences on your resume

Volunteering is a job, whether you get paid for it or not. And, it certainly is better than telling your interviewer that you were sitting at home catching up on your soap operas. Volunteer opportunities can fill in some of the gaps on your resume.

Volunteers tend to have good job karma

Remember back in the days when you were dating? How many more people asked you on a date as soon as you started seeing someone else? I rest my case.

Volunteering brings you natural joy because you are helping others

Just think about how you feel when you lift someone up who falls, or when you help a co-worker solve a problem, or when you help a child with his homework. Happier people land jobs faster because they exude positive energy and passion.

If you're not sure where to start, just think of your hobbies. If you enjoy sports, coach at a YMCA. If you like to sing, manage a glee club. If you like animals, volunteer at a shelter. Organize a church group, paint schools, build houses, feed the homeless…you get the picture. Visit Idealist.org or VolunteerMatch.org where you'll find plenty of ways to get started.

> **Absolutely Abby's Advice:** *Volunteering is a great way to fill gaps in employment while also broadening your network and potentially increasing your chances of landing quickly. Most of all have fun with it! It can be the experience of a lifetime if you choose with your heart.*

66

▪ 38 ▪ Be a Career Fair Keeper

Career fairs can be beneficial events to attend because you can make many employment connections in one day, but as in all other phases of the job search process, preparation is the key to success. You can find career fairs in the United States at www.LocalHires.com.

A career fair, like a networking event is an interview in disguise. You have 30 seconds or less to tell the recruiter about yourself, quickly capture their attention, and entice them to want to learn more. "Yes", "No", and "Maybe" decisions are made about you on the spot. Typically recruiters have three piles – the "Keepers", the "I don't know what to do with this person but I like them for something" pile, and the "I'm really not sure what this person was thinking" pile. Let's review the top ten ways to improve your odds of landing in the first pile.

1) Dress like you are going to an interview. A professional image leaves recruiters with a positive impression and will also improve your self-confidence, which is a must at a career fair.

2) Bring at least 50 resumes printed on special quality resume paper. Running out of copies before the day is over won't get you into the Keepers pile.

3) Do your homework before the event. Research the companies on the roster, and see which positions they typically hire for. Be prepared to speak with companies about specific roles that you might fit into, regardless of whether they are currently open.

4) Prepare a short introductory statement about yourself ahead of time. Find a way to tell a recruiter what you are all about in 30 seconds or less and then end with a closing question such as, "would someone with my background be a good fit for your organization?"

5) Make sure that your breath smells fresh as the day continues. You have less than one minute to make an impression – make a good one!

6) Maintain good eye contact with the recruiter, and remember to smile! Smiling is contagious and if you're smiling, you'll both remember the experience more positively. Also be sure to offer a firm handshake.

7) Avoid asking the question "What positions are you recruiting for?" Instead, be prepared to talk about what you can offer to the company and let them tell you what positions they have that might match your background.

8) Ask each person for their business card and don't be surprised if recruiters "don't have any" or "ran out". Business cards might suddenly appear if you are a top candidate. If the recruiter does not offer you a card, at least ask for the correct spelling of his or her name. If you end up with a pile of business cards that have actual names on them, rather than generic ones, consider yourself to have had a very successful day.

9) Try to visit each booth even if you don't think they have positions that match your background. You never know which unadvertised positions recruiters have up their sleeves. Plus, it's a great networking opportunity and provides you with practice delivering your elevator pitch. Recruiters that have shorter lines will have more time to speak with you individually.

10) The day after the event, e-mail thank you notes to the recruiters you met. This is your chance to quickly remind them about your conversation and to differentiate yourself from the crowd. Less than 1% of candidates ever follow up, so this is an easy way to make yourself known.

> ***Absolutely Abby's Advice:*** *By attending a career fair, you can learn a great deal about specific employers, practice effective networking, and perfect your elevator pitch. The key to success at a career fair is being prepared. So, do your homework, put on some comfortable shoes and then get out there!*

▪ 39 ▪ Being a Good Sport

Whether you are a sports enthusiast or simply watch the Super Bowl for the commercials, most of you have participated in a team sport in the past, even if it was just in high school gym class. Sports can play an important part in your career in the form of leadership experience on your resume, as an interim activity while you search, or simply as an abundance of lessons learned.

If you are currently faced with extra time on your hands, consider playing on, managing, or coaching a sports team. Here are some lessons that you can learn from sports that can easily be extrapolated into your life and career.

1) Teamwork – By now I am sure that you've heard the statement, "There's no "I" in team". In sports, you learn to get along with a variety of people who are all on the team for the same reason. Playing on a team teaches you the importance of setting goals and then working together to achieve them. No matter what job you are in, being a team player is a frequent requirement.

2) Rules – Team sports have rules and, in the workplace, breaking rules usually has greater consequences than in other areas of your life. In the workplace, some rules are bendable, but make sure that you know which ones they are.

3) Winning is Better Than Losing – If you are a competitive person, you always want to win the game, but hopefully not at any cost.

For instance, you want to win by playing fair, but not by cheating. In the workplace, being competitive can cost you both friendships and respect, so while you want to win, it's important to understand the political ramifications and plan accordingly.

4) Losing Isn't as Bad as You Think It Is – When you lose a game, your coach guides you towards improving your game for the next time. The same goes for your job responsibilities. Sometimes you succeed and other times your performance needs some tweaking. Mistakes help you learn. If you were absolutely perfect, life would be boring.

5) Leadership – If you have been a team captain, even if it was a long time ago, it is still a beneficial addition to your resume. Being elected or anointed captain is an honor which is readily acknowledged by recruiters as true leadership experience.

Absolutely Abby's Advice: Team sports teach us a variety of life lessons that are easily adaptable to your career. They also offer excellent networking opportunities and companionship and play a role in stress management and fitness. You may have cobwebs on your volleyball, soccer ball, tennis racket, baseball glove or football, but once you dust them off, the desire you once had to join the team will resurface faster than you thought possible.

▪ 40 ▪ A Jobseeker's GPS

A networking connection of mine once wrote an interesting comment on her Facebook page: "It amazes me that if I put an address in my GPS, and do exactly what it says, I actually get to my destination!"

Wouldn't it be nice if there was a job search GPS and if you did exactly what it told you to do that you would land the job of your dreams? As you know, life just isn't that controllable.

If you had a job search GPS, it might give you instructions for a perfectly acceptable route – but it might not be the best one for you. Different candidates may need to take alternate routes in order to arrive at their ultimate destination. Unique strategies are required for different industries and positions. There is not one exact way to write a resume, one way to interview or one way to find a job. There are many. Your job search GPS would get mighty confused over the one page versus multiple page resume debate, the wear a suit versus match the company's dress code debate, and the use LinkedIn versus Facebook debate. Your success will come from listening to what all the experts say and then developing a plan that seems right for you.

One way to make your job search not as daunting is to plan it out in small steps, each resulting in a goal that you can be proud of when it has been reached. Choose to attend one career seminar or networking event each week or choose to send out a certain number of resumes. Make five calls to new headhunters or find 30 more connections on LinkedIn. Set a goal to have one interview every week, whether on the phone or live. Congratulate yourself and celebrate when you hit these targets. Look at them as rest stops along the highway of life.

To get to your ultimate goal…your new job…you may very well have to make some difficult choices along the way. You may have to accept a role that is not quite what you anticipated to get your foot into the door of your ideal company. You may have to settle for a lower title that you had in your last position to keep your commute manageable. You may even need to accept a decrease in pay to start in an industry that better fuels your passion. But, if you choose to make the most of your decision, to learn as much as you can from your new experiences, and to choose to put a positive spin on the cards you are dealt, you will ultimately find life to be that much more rewarding.

Absolutely Abby's Advice: *A job search takes you down a path that may seem unfamiliar to you at first, but eventually, you will find that it is just another part of the journey of your life's work. It is a road for which there is no GPS, but once you reach your destination, you will feel the greatest sense of satisfaction for having traveled it.*

Dare to Be Different

▪ 41 ▪ Differentiating Yourself From the Flock

One day I discovered a lesson in job seeking as I was feeding a bunch of swans in a large pond in Brooklyn. Those of you, who live in big cities where swans exist only on greeting cards, might better be able to relate to the experience if you think of feeding a flock of pigeons. Or, if you've spent time in Australia, think of the joy of feeding a troop of kangaroos. Now how could this possibly be a lesson for jobseekers, you ask? Stay tuned.

The animal kingdom survives by mirroring. If one animal sees food, he slowly approaches it and then attacks. The others naturally follow in the same way. As humans we tend to work in a similar fashion. We listen to the strategies that other people are using to find and apply for jobs and we follow the same course of action. We figure that what works for someone else, should also work for us.

The problem with this approach is competition. The swans were huddled together and were all fighting for the same loaf of bread I was feeding them. The swans who were larger and stronger were able to find more bread , while others did not get any at all.

These days, you're going to have to do things differently than the flock in order to get noticed! Here are three ideas:

1) Sign up for all the job search related Yahoo Groups you can find at groups.yahoo.com by searching for the keywords job, jobs, and leads. To narrow your search to your industry, use "job pharmaceutical" for example. To narrow the search to your city, use "leads Las Vegas". While you're there, join my Yahoo group "AbsolutelyJobLeads". Now here's where you can be different than the flock. Don't just join the groups. Be different than the

flock by contributing leads that you aren't planning to follow through with to your group. When you meet your peers in person at a live event one day, they will already know who you are.

2) Start a blog and/or join the Twitterverse to help the world understand a little bit more about you. Blog or tweet about challenges in your industry and give your opinions about how you might fix them. Consider partnering up with someone who can proofread your posts for both grammar and tone and also to help you brainstorm new ideas.

3) Realize that any time you spend with others is networking. Attending in-transition groups is certainly a good first step, but there are so many other ways for you to meet people including at the gym, at a workshop or industry seminar, at church, at the supermarket, on a plane, at a party, on the bleachers at a baseball game, at a volunteer event…this list could go on for days. Leave the comfort of your home as often as possible and start talking to more people who can point you in the right direction.

Absolutely Abby's Advice: *In the past, just being one of the flock may have been good enough. You would apply for 15 jobs, have 5 interviews and get 2 offers with negotiable salaries and bonuses. Times have changed. In this day and age, it takes out of the box thinking to get an edge on the competition. People who take chances will be rewarded. Fed ex your resume, drop off your resume by hand, and use other creative ways to get noticed. Before long, you will be singing your job search swan song.*

▪ 42 ▪ The Museum of Old Technology

These days there are many new ways of forwarding your resume to a company – most of which involve a computer. We have online applications, online resumes, and online networking. Sometimes differentiating yourself is as easy as turning back the clock.

I remember the 90's well. I used to ride the bus back and forth to work every day, accompanied by a stack of at least 200 resumes. I would flip through them one by one looking for those perfect candidates, who I couldn't wait to call the next morning. These days, the old fashioned metal mailbox in the Human Resources department tends to be very lonely because the only mail we receive is invoices, new product advertisements and miscellaneous propaganda. Seeing a resume printed on bond paper every once in a while, complete with a well-written cover letter, would be a breath of fresh air. Do you think I would risk a paper cut and open it? Absolutely!

Fax machines around the country are lonely as well. They are no longer the most used piece of office equipment as they have given that title away to their cousin, the computer. I remember looking forward to Monday mornings to see piles of faxed resumes in response to my newspaper ads. So why not fax your resume to the lonely fax machine? It's a great way to make sure that someone is going to actually read it. While you're at it, apply online as well so that you have two chances of being seen and so that you're not seen as a rebel who cannot follow directions.

The last piece of antiquated equipment to bring back to life is the telephone. With text messaging and e-mail becoming so prevalent, Alexander Graham Bell's famous invention has become a dinosaur in itself. Not so for my friend Bob who I bumped into at a networking event a few months ago. A headhunter placed an ad for a Purchasing Agent and Bob was one of 500 people who applied online for the job. Bob knew that he was the perfect candidate – the job description seemed as if it was taken directly from his resume. Bob waited for a few days, and then called the headhunter to check on his application. The headhunter was glad that Bob called because she didn't have time to look at all 500 resumes. While she had Bob on the phone, she screened him for the position and decided

75

to send him in the next day to meet with the company. Bob landed the job in one week after making his phone call. Not all phone call attempts will work out as well. Also remember that calling is one thing, but stalking is another.

> **Absolutely Abby's Advice:** *In any economy, you must do things differently than your competition to get noticed. Can I guarantee you that the mailed in or faxed resumes will be read, or that the phone call will be taken seriously every time? Absolutely not. But I can promise you that persistence and out of the box thinking will keep you miles ahead of your competition.*

▪ 43 ▪ Warming Up The Cold Call

For many people, public speaking is their greatest fear. In most cases, it even beats the fear of dying. A close runner up is the fear of cold calling a prospective employer.

A cold call is NOT defined as a call placed on the ski slopes in Switzerland. "Cold calling" is the process of approaching prospective customers or clients, typically via telephone, who were not expecting such an interaction. The word "cold" is used because the person receiving the call is not expecting a call or has not specifically asked to be contacted by the person.

When you call a prospective employer on the phone, is that really a cold call? Absolutely! It's just as cold as if you were calling to ask them to vote in the election, or if you were calling to ask them to donate to your charity. Why? Because when you call, you are asking them to buy something…and the something you are selling is YOU!

So why on earth would any reasonable person (except the bold among us with sales experience) ever consider making such calls? Good question. Here's why: (1) very few candidates are actually using this approach –

because it is such a scary proposition, and (2) because cold calls can work wonders when handled correctly!

The best way to ensure success is to warm up the cold call by letting the person know beforehand that you are going to make the call. There are many ways to do this:

1) You can send them a note of introduction via LinkedIn

2) You can find someone who knows both of you to recommend you

3) You can send them an e-mail

4) You can send them a letter in the mail

5) You can fax them a letter

6) You can send them a letter via Fed Ex. Now why would you want to spend this extra money? Based on a largely unscientific study, I've found that 99% of the working population opens their own overnight mail, regardless of who sent it.

7) Your note should contain a sentence like this, "I will call you on X date at X time to discuss setting a time for us to discuss my letter."

To get an interview, for a job that they may or may not have open, you will need to illustrate that you are someone who can solve a problem they have. That means that you need to do plenty of research beforehand to determine what problems exist in the organization as a whole.

I recommend calling before 9AM or after 5PM so that the Executive Assistants who would normally block the call have left the building like Elvis. I also recommend blocking your caller-ID and then calling back later rather than leaving a voicemail message. Just don't overdo it by calling too many times because their phone is still ringing every time you dial.

When the prospective employer answers, don't ask whether they received your letter. Assume they did. Start with, "I sent you a letter earlier this week and I am following up as I stated I would. I have ABC experience and am interested in discussing how my experience can help bring XYZ value to your organization. Would Monday or Tuesday afternoon work for a 15 minute informational interview?"

Role-play this conversation with a friend until you can say it with confidence, and then, go for it. You don't need 100 people to agree to see you. Oftentimes, all it takes is one person who is so impressed by how far out of the box you have traveled, that they not only interview you, but also decide to hire you.

> **Absolutely Abby's Advice:** *It's a rare bird who enjoys cold calling, but it's something different to try. What do you have to lose? The worst they can say is no. The best-case scenario is that you will catch them at the perfect time, and they will not be able to reject you because you actually do have a solution to their problem. Just think, once you master cold calling, public speaking won't seem half as bad.*

▪ 44 ▪ For Your Information: Informational Interviews

An "Informational Interview" is a meeting in which you ask for advice rather than employment. The goal is to gather information about a specific profession or industry, find employment leads, and expand your professional network. This differs from a job interview because you are initiating the interview and asking the questions. And, there may or may not be employment opportunities available.

No matter what stage of career development you are at, asking for an opportunity to meet with an expert inside the walls of a company that you might want to work for someday is a tool in your toolbox worth dusting off.

Before the informational interview, prepare a list of questions about the person's career and about the career opportunities available in the industry and/or specific company. To help you create intelligent questions, Google the person and research the company as you would do for a traditional interview. Organize your questions so that the first ones are the most critical for expanding your knowledge. You may not have the opportunity to ask more than a few prepared questions, so plan your strategy wisely. The key is to end at the agreed time, regardless of how many questions were asked.

Here are 10 questions you might ask, but not necessarily in this order:

1) What does a typical day at your job involve? What are your main responsibilities?

2) What responsibilities do you enjoy most?

3) What challenges do you face in your job?

4) Why did you choose this field? Why did you choose this job? How did you get started?

5) What were the most important steps you took that led you to the job that you have now?

6) What is the best way to gain the experience that I need for this field?

7) What do you think about your industry? Do you like it more or less than others you have been working in?

8) What other roles can you fill with your background?

9) What other kinds of people are hired in this company/industry?

10) Why did you decide to work for this company? What do you like most? Least?

The questions should be personal and career related, rather than questions that you would ask if you were applying for a specific job.

Here are several additional tips to help make your informational interview a smashing success:

✓ Dress for success as if you were on a real interview. In many cases, an informational interview can turn quickly into a real one, if the person on the other side of the desk determines that you might be able to fill a current need.

✓ Respect the interviewer's time. End the interview when you promised to, and be pleased if the person offers you the opportunity to continue the conversation. People Absolutely love to talk about themselves and their career, so they are typically very willing to provide a wealth of information. The time will fly by and you'll both probably wish that you could keep talking forever, but alas, the time will eventually come to say goodbye.

✓ At the conclusion of the interview, ask for a business card and more importantly, ask if he or she would mind if you kept in touch. As you would with a networking contact, ask for names and contact information of people who you might network further with. If you're lucky, one of these people may become your new boss.

✓ As with a regular interview, write a spectacular thank you note. Tell the person how much you appreciated their time and give specific reasons why the information they provided was valuable.

Informational interviews can also happen informally at networking events – good reason number 857 for attending them. For example, while you are introducing yourself to a fellow attendee, you may discover that he is in the job, the industry, or the company that you are also interested in. If he obliges, ask several questions at the event, and then offer to buy the person coffee afterwards so that you can pick his brain a bit more. Very few people will turn down an opportunity to talk about themselves, especially if it includes a free meal.

> **Absolutely Abby's Advice:** *Despite the fact that the informational interview has the word "interview" in it, you should not expect that it will turn into a job offer. What you should expect is that you will gain a wealth of knowledge that can move you several steps down your path towards your new job. If you are someone who aspires to greatness every step of the way, and someone who loves to learn, the informational interview may very well become your new best friend.*

▪ 45 ▪ The Entrepreneurial You

Dating back almost as far as when I left the womb, I've always wanted to start my own business. It started with the typical lemonade stand on my front porch in Brooklyn and then continued with the carnival I created for the neighborhood kids in my driveway. I'm not exactly sure, but I think I may have tried to sell snow one winter. Trust me…there's a business idea in all of us…some of us just have to reach a little deeper down to find it.

These days, because of the web, starting your own business is simple and inexpensive. It can literally happen in minutes! However, maintaining, marketing, and funding it is another story entirely, but there are many resources that can help you with that. One example is SCORE (www.score.org), a nonprofit association dedicated to educating entrepreneurs on the formation, growth and success of small business. SCORE has 370 chapters throughout the United States with 11,200 volunteers nationwide. Both working and retired executives and business owners donate time and expertise as business counselors.

To start a business, the first two things you need to know are what you excel at and what you love to do. There have been many helpful books written on the subject such as "Finding Your True Calling" and "Do What You Love and The Money Will Follow".

Once you choose your business idea, there will obviously be business expenses to contend with, but there will also be plenty of deductions that you can take. All businesses have start up costs but some are less than $500.

The best part about having your own business is just that…it's YOUR BUSINESS. That is, you no longer have to worry about getting laid off, downsized, right-sized, reorganized, or whatever else the media chooses to call it. Nothing is perfect as you know, and running a business has its own special nuances associated with it, but at the same time, it can be the perfect choice for someone with an entrepreneurial personality.

> ***Absolutely Abby's Advice:*** *The most important thing about starting a business is this: it should revolve around the thing or idea that you are most passionate about. It should be something you can't wait to get up in the morning to do. It should be something that you lie awake at night daydreaming about. It should be something that you would be willing to do for free if you were independently wealthy. Choosing wisely and then staying motivated during the rough patches will be a key to your success.*

▪ 46 ▪ The Zero Experience Factor

All around you, people are landing in jobs with less than half of the required qualifications written on the job description. Is it magic? Is it luck? Is it some sort of voodoo that gets these job stealers hired with far less qualifications that you have? In some cases, maybe, but I'd be willing to bet that for 99.9% of them, it's their winning attitude and their motivation.

This recently happened to a friend of mine who I'll call Linda. Linda graduated from college this past May and was ready to find her first job. She was a psychology honors student and was also the captain of her college volleyball team. In thinking about her career aspirations, Linda decided that a career in Human Resources would be perfect for her because she loved helping people. She began looking for positions.

The summer zoomed by, and although Linda had a wonderful resume for a recent college graduate, she was far from a perfect candidate for a Human Resources position, as she had no experience. This became quite obvious as the negative responses came pouring in from the ads that she was answering. But, Linda didn't give up. She started thinking outside the box, and that's when she began to take these actions steps:

1) She wrote an extraordinary cover letter and mailed it to small company CEO's whose names she found on Google and LinkedIn. In the letter, she mentioned that she was looking for an internship rather than a job.

2) She started attending networking events to meet Human Resources professionals who might be able to help her get her foot in the door.

3) She volunteered at Habitat for Humanity and made oodles of great connections.

4) She went to happy hours in New York City with her friends, hoping to bump into Human Resources professionals from companies in the neighborhood.

5) She started a blog to introduce herself and to display her intelligence to the world.

A Vice President of Human Resources for a major publisher happened to read her blog. That's when things started happening.

Linda received a call from the Vice President and was invited in for an exploratory interview. The Vice President honestly had no idea how specifically she might help Linda, but she felt that she needed to meet the person who blogged with such passion and eloquence. When the Vice President met Linda, she was instantly impressed by her drive, motivation, and knowledge of current Human Resources issues. Linda started work two weeks later as the Vice President's Administrative Assistant. Linda didn't need a magician — she created her own magic.

> ***Absolutely Abby's Advice:*** *People hire people, not resumes. The lucky "landers" are strong interviewers with loads of confidence and dynamic personalities. They are people who have learned to differentiate themselves from the crowd, and they are excellent networkers. Improve your interview skills and you will improve your success rate to the nth degree.*

▪ 47 ▪ Unlocking the Secret to Your Success

Brian Tracy, a motivational speaker once said, "Life is like a combination lock; your job is to find the numbers, in the right orders so you can have anything you want." Here are two stories about people who found some interesting things to do with their time in transition, which became the perfect combination.

Joe was a help desk technician and had been working in the financial services industry for the past 25 years. He had all the important certifications and was continuously a star performer. Joe also had a special knack of fixing the customer first, a skill he was taught early on in his career. But…Joe felt that something was missing. As much as he enjoyed working in financial services, his dream was to work for a company that helped people in a different way. He chose healthcare…but healthcare would not choose him.

As I'm sure you know well by now, certain industries look for candidates with experience in the same industry. As much as you think that marketing is marketing, finance is finance, and IT is IT, many industry leaders don't always agree. Joe sent out 25 resumes to hospitals and didn't receive one phone call.

Joe realized he needed to start thinking outside the box. He decided to volunteer at a hospital on the days that he was not interviewing or attending networking events. If he couldn't work in healthcare, at least he could still find a way to help people. Slowly but surely, Joe developed connections with the hospital administrators while fixing their computers.

Eventually Joe received an offer at a new financial services firm for a higher paying job that required more hours. When he mentioned that he would be leaving the hospital, the Chief Administrative Officer asked him not to. Suddenly, a position was created with Joe's name on it, much to his delight.

Another friend of mine, who I will call Jim, told a different story. Jim was a marketing executive in the manufacturing industry for 20 years until his position was eliminated, much to his surprise. To have a successful interview, a marketing professional must have confidence seeping out of each and every pore. Unfortunately Jim's confidence was below sea level thanks to the layoff. To build his confidence, Jim decided to take ballroom dancing lessons, not because this was something he always wanted to do, but because it was something he never thought he could master. Jim told me that his friends teased him about his coordination and grace any time they saw him dance.

Jim took lessons three nights a week for several months along with a class of nine other people. Now, you're probably thinking that Jim landed a job because he was hired by someone taking the class, but as interesting of an ending as that would be, that is not what happened to Jim.

Not only did Jim become a ballroom dancer, but his friends were envious as he waltzed around the room at weddings. He was exceptional, and he far surpassed even his own expectations. Jim told me that his newfound confidence in himself helped him become a much stronger interviewer as he started to believe and portray to hiring managers that no matter what the challenge, he could overcome it. Jim is now happily employed again as a Director of Marketing in the manufacturing industry.

> ***Absolutely Abby's Advice:*** *Unless you have psychic powers, you will not know what activities, events or connections will ultimately lead you to landing on your feet in your next job. Thinking way outside the box will suit you well, amidst all the competition. Become involved in activities that you enjoy and use sites like Meetup.com or Eventme.com to connect with other people that have similar interests. Each week, turn the dial on your life's combination lock to a new number, and eventually you will unlock the secret to your success.*

▪ 48 ▪ Out of The Box Thinking

Here are two success stories that are more out of this world than out of the box.

My friend Karl, an attorney, had been searching for a position for several months, and so far had come up empty handed. One day he saw an ad on Monster for a position at a manufacturer. Karl read the ad and then gasped at the closing line. The company had written a statement that could be seen as discriminatory if read in a certain way.

Without thinking twice, Karl knew what he had to do. He climbed into his car and drove to the company's headquarters. He asked the receptionist if he could see the hiring manager for the position, and then proceeded to describe the error in the ad. The hiring manager was so grateful, he invited Karl in for an interview. Karl was hired two months later.

Could Karl have just called the company? Yes. Could he have just addressed the error in his cover letter? Yes. Could the hiring manager have been disinterested or turned off by Karl? Yes, but sometimes you just have to take a chance in life with so many other jobseekers in your midst.

The second story is about Raina who was downsized from a job in Human Resources. Rather than dwell on her downfall, Raina developed new goals for herself and then began to blog about them. She wrote about all the wonderful things to do for free in New York City and then set out to complete each one. She ran a marathon, fished in Central Park and toured the United Nations. All of a sudden, someone noticed Raina's blog. That someone was a CNN reporter and Raina's story ran on TV. Raina is now employed as an HR Coordinator for a large bank. She is still continuing to blog and uncovers new things to do in New York City on the weekends.

> *Absolutely Abby's Advice:* Thinking outside the box is way more important now than it was in the past few years. Creative thinkers will be rewarded by an abundance of opportunities that never even appear as a blip on the average person's radar screen. Think creatively, take chances, and get hired!

▪ 49 ▪   The Business of Business Cards

Anybody who is actively searching for a job typically makes at least one or two appearances per month at an networking event, which may be called an "in-transition group", a job search group, or a career networking group.

When you travel around to these networking groups, it is important to hand your new connections a piece of personal collateral, which, like your resume, represents your career brand. Enter the business card!

When someone is trying to find you quickly to share a job lead or to ask you for help making a connection, your business card is a critical piece of the puzzle. While you can just use your business card from a current employer (when you are employed), consider the value of creating a personal card for networking purposes. Your card should obviously have key details about you, such as your name and contact information, but there are a variety of other things that you can do to separate yourself from the crowd:

1) Your card should represent you – if you are a vibrant, exuberant person, you may want to choose a colorful template for your card. Let your card represent your own personal style.

2) Your card design may be different based on your industry or profession. For example, engineers and accountants might opt for a more traditional card, while marketing and sales professionals might choose a more flashy background.

3) Your goal as both a networker and a candidate is to be memorable. Consider adding a list of skills that differentiate you from your competition to your business card. This will help

fellow networkers and interviewers remember you easily without having to look up your information.

4) There are many free business card services on the web where printers put their name on the back of your card as a form of advertising. While this may save you a few dollars, some recruiters will perceive this as less than professional. Additionally, these free business cards are limited to a small subset of design templates so there is a greater chance that your card will end up looking like someone else's. Similar to wearing the same dress at the prom, you do not want to have the same card that your new connection has. Investing $30 for custom-made cards is well worth the investment.

5) If you choose to print your cards at home, consider that the person you hand them to will probably be able to tell. Cards that are printed at home typically have slightly jagged edges and significantly thinner paper than traditionally printed cards. If you use an inkjet printer, the text will not look as sharp. Consider having your cards printed by a printing company to complement your professional image.

6) If you decide to put a picture of yourself on your card, make sure that it is a professional photo. Digital cameras are everywhere nowadays so this should be a simple task. Remember that this card may be passed among many people so it is critical that you look your best. But, don't feel that you need your picture on your card. Most people don't add them.

7) If you have a choice of coatings such as "UV" or "aqueous" on your card, you should keep the back side uncoated so that people can jot down notes on your card after they meet you. Your printer may describe the lack of a coating as "matte" or "dull".

8) Your card is *your* card whether you are employed or not. This card can be used at networking events before and after you start your new job, so do not indicate whether you are employed or not on the card.

Let's get back to business by looking at the back of these itty-bitty pieces of collateral. The front of your card is obviously extremely important, especially if it the only side with information on it. However, these days, there are several creative ways to add finesse to your back side.

1) List of Skills – Create a bulleted list of skills that you can offer to the company. For example, an Administrative Assistant might list these skills:

   ▪ Word processing
   ▪ Spreadsheets
   ▪ PowerPoint presentations
   ▪ Travel arrangements
   ▪ Social Media
   ▪ 55 WPM typing

2) List of References – A good friend of mine titled the back of his card with "What former managers have said" and then proceeded to list their testimonials:

   ▪ Superb listener
   ▪ Articulate communicator
   ▪ Analytical contributor
   ▪ Creative thinker
   ▪ Fantastic leader and mentor
   ▪ A man of courage

3) Contact Information – Typically the front of your card can get crowded so you can use the back of your card to list links to your Twitter, Facebook, LinkedIn, and other social media profiles.

4) Your Objective – Listing your objective on the back of the card enables people to remember exactly who you are, and more importantly, how they can help connect you.

> **Absolutely Abby's Advice:** *Everything you do, say, and write is being evaluated at all times when you're communicating with people, especially when you are searching for a job. Your business card, or lack thereof is one of those items that you will be judged on, so it is critical that it represents the most professional you. Create a card that you can be proud of and it will automatically enhance your confidence when you hand it out. And confidence is clearly the way to win the prize!*

▪ 50 ▪ The Successful Pitcher

At most networking events that you attend, you will typically be asked to give a 30 second "elevator pitch". The elevator pitch is a personal branding testimonial that differentiates you from your peers. It positions you as a leader in your field who can fill a particular niche in the workplace better than anyone else. In short it is your "value proposition" and it markets you to your next employer.

Your pitch should be a concise, carefully planned, and well-practiced description about your past and future employment, which your mother should be able to understand and remember in the time it would take to ride on an elevator. Let's review this in more detail:

Your elevator pitch must be concise

If you are in an elevator or at a networking group or on line at the supermarket, the people that you meet don't necessarily have time to hear your entire career history, especially if you end it with a plea for a new job. What they might want to learn is what makes you so valuable to an employer that IF they had a job available that matched your profile, they would want to hire you. And you typically should aim to do that in 30 seconds or less.

Your elevator pitch must be memorable

Your pitch should have some sort of "hook" in it so that it triggers a memory about you. My friend Al, a Vice President of Advertising for a large firm, delivered the best hook I remember. The last line of his elevator pitch was, "when you hire Al Adams, you get an A in Advertising".

Your elevator pitch must be carefully planned

Your pitch should include statements about your accomplishments and, if possible, should quantify these accomplishments. For example, "in my last position, I was able to reduce operating expenses by 25%" or, "in my role as the Vice President of Sales, I led a team who more than tripled the sales quota".

Your elevator pitch is a "pitch" for an opportunity

Think of your pitch as your 30 second commercial in which your goal is to keep your audience entertained. You must be able to ask for the help that you need, but not in a presumptuous manner. Something simple like this will do, "I am seeking an opportunity at a pharmaceutical company where I can use my strengths in clinical research to evaluate new products."

Your pitch must be something your mother would be able to understand

Most of the time, the person hearing your pitch will not be your future boss (or your mother). But, it could certainly be your neighbor, your son's friend's father, or your networking buddy, who will most likely not understand what you do, even after you have explained it to them. Your pitch should not include technical terms of any kind – it should include very basic language. The fact is that is doesn't really matter if people understand the details of what you do. They just have to understand the kinds of people to refer you to, should they have the opportunity to do so. That is the entire essence of the elevator pitch…simple and memorable.

Once you have your pitch written, practice it until the pitch becomes a part of who you are, so much so that it just rolls off your tongue. You can read it from a cheat sheet while at a networking event. But, you'll come across as having more zeal for what you do if you have your pitch rehearsed and memorized, so when the opportunity presents itself in a real life situation, you'll be ready!

> **Absolutely Abby's Advice:** *An elevator pitch is your chance to tell anyone that you meet what you're all about in short order. Sometimes you'll have 30 seconds and sometimes you'll have five minutes. The key is to get the point across that you are someone who should Absolutely be recommended for an opportunity. If you can accomplish that, you are well on your way!*

▪ 51 ▪ The Nuances of Networking

Is it good enough just to attend a networking event or is there really more magic required? The answer is that there is.

The magic is all about you. You create the success of the event, as opposed to relying on everyone else around you to create it. Simply put, you get out what you put in, and in some cases, you get so much more.

The most important thing to realize about networking is that almost everyone is nervous, regardless of how many events they have attended in the past. As you enter the room, notice the people that look like deer gazing into the headlights. That person is sometimes going to be you. So then, how can you turn this nervous energy into success? It's simple – just start asking questions.

Find someone who looks as scared as you feel and walk right up to them. Ask them their name, rank & serial number (or just their name), and then ask them if they live or work in the area or if they have been to the group before or whether they know anyone else in the room. This kind of small talk will put both of you at ease.

After the conversation gets going, you can begin to ask some more involved questions such as "What industry do you work in?" or "What kinds of positions are you looking for?" or "What are your target companies?" Asking questions will make the person believe that you really care about helping them, and that, my friends, is the key to "paying it forward".

Once your networking buddy answers all of your questions, he or she will start asking questions about you. This is a key point in your conversation. Based on the time you have available, you should be delivering your well-planned, well-rehearsed elevator pitch. In the same way that you have 10 seconds to get a recruiter to like your resume, you only have a few seconds to get someone to understand you via your elevator pitch. If your pitch is not memorable, or if it's dry and boring, your voice will blend in with the noise of the event, and your buddy won't make the connection when he or she meets someone else who has a lead that might help you.

> **Abby's Absolute Advice:** *Anyone, including an introvert, can learn to be a networker, and can even learn to enjoy it! So many of my closest friendships resulted from a deer in the headlights journey into a scary room where I knew no one. Networking is not just recommended for job search success – it is an Absolute requirement. Be brave, show your pearly whites, and let's go out and network together!*

▪ 52 ▪ The Elementary Rules of Networking

The interesting thing about networking is that we all know how to do it successfully…we just forgot how young we were when we learned. Think back to elementary school. Can you remember the first day when your mom dropped you off? Regardless of your personality, I guarantee that you were Absolutely terrified. But you somehow figured out how to make friends. You found kids who had similar interests and you spent the most time with them. You were networking back then but you didn't even know it.

Today, networking could not be more important. Everyone including Oprah is talking about it. It's everywhere you look. When the race between Ashton Kutcher and CNN for the #1 Twitter ranking made national headlines, you can be sure that you needed to start paying attention.

Networking is really simple…it's all about making new friends like you did in school. The problem is that like pushy used car salesmen, some "networkers" have given networking a bad reputation. Let's review some key DO's and DON'Ts about networking:

DON'T just walk around handing out your business cards by the dozens.

DO exchange business cards with anyone you meet with whom you have a genuine interest in staying in touch.

DON'T expect all of the "networking" to happen during the networking event.

DO follow-up with people you met after the event and discuss how you might be able to help each other pay it forward. The more you can give others, the more others will naturally want to help you. Networking is a two-way street.

DON'T expect networking to work for you if all you do is call your old friends, managers and colleagues only when you need something from them.

DO call the people you have lost touch with and reconnect with them for the purposes of re-establishing a strong relationship. Sites like LinkedIn and Facebook make it really easy to keep in touch with friends, even if all you do is drop them a fast hello every so often. There is no longer any excuse not to stay connected.

> *Absolutely Abby's Advice: The next time that you are at a networking event, think of the attendees as potential friends, not people who can do things for you. Ask people about their hobbies, their family, and their favorite vacation spots, not just about their career. While it might feel uncomfortable at first, it will soon become as natural as tying your shoes. And over time, you will meet some of the world's most inspiring, motivating, helpful people who you might even call your friends. Your first grade self will be very proud of you!*

▪ 53 ▪ E is for Etiquette

Communication is everything when it comes to networking. Bad etiquette results in bad feelings whereas good etiquette results in positive reinforcement, and therefore a continuation of the same behaviors occurring in the future. Here are several aspects of networking etiquette that you should strive to master:

Time Etiquette

Be respectful of the amount of time you are allocating for conversations. If you are referred or recommended to someone, ask the person if they have a few minutes to speak with you rather than launching into a 15-minute monologue. At a networking event, do not spend too much time with any one person, especially if you already know them. Make an effort to meet several people at each event for a short amount of time, and then schedule follow up meetings after the events with those where mutual interest is established.

Feedback Etiquette

If someone refers or recommends you to someone, make every effort to keep them in the loop as the communications unfold. Your contacts will appreciate knowing that their advice or direction was helpful.

Follow Up Etiquette

Always say what you are going to do and then do it. If you say that you are going to follow up, do it. If you say that you are going to call at 3PM, do it. If you are late or need to cancel the appointment, it's fine, as long as you provide a reason. People understand when things come up

E-mail Etiquette

Make every attempt to say the two most underutilized words in the dictionary, according to me... thank you! If someone sends out a job lead and you decide to follow up on it, why not drop them a line to thank them for sharing it. It will encourage them to share more in the future.

Gratitude Etiquette

If someone does something for you that helps your job search, even if it's only a small thing, thank him or her. If they help you with your resume, share their work experience in an industry you are targeting, or if they coach you through a situation, thank them by writing them a note, a recommendation on LinkedIn or a testimonial. That will only encourage them to help you and others even more.

It's never too late to thank someone who helped you. In that vein, I hereby thank my former bosses for having extremely high standards when it comes to written documents. It's because of you that I can now find those persnickety little errors on people's resumes and how I developed my writing skills to write this book. And, thank you to all of the networking experts who I met along the way that taught me all of the other components above. My heart goes out to each and every one of you! Thank you. Thank you. Thank you!

> ***Absolutely Abby's Advice:*** *Networking is about building new bridges. Strive to meet new people in every situation you encounter. However, don't neglect the people that you already know. Building strong bridges rather than burning them is a key to your success.*

▪ 54 ▪ Network Easy

Since everyone, including me, recommends that you network like crazy nowadays, the question is, how do you keep up with all of it, especially if networking does not come naturally for you?

Sure, networking seems easy. It's about meeting new people, sharing what's on your mind, and then figuring out how you can help them with whatever they are working on at the time. Alas…what's easy for some is not easy for all. Some people enjoy networking and are at ease when making new connections. For others, it takes work to summon up the courage to attend an event when they don't expect to know anyone else there. That tension can cause you to want to take a break from networking events every once in a while.

Remember that anytime you are having a conversation, you are networking. Talking to your friends, talking to your family and talking to the person next to you on the plane, is networking. You are simply getting to know people better than you knew them before and trying to help them achieve their goals, no matter how small. So even if you take a break

99

from the formal events, spend time with friends and family and brainstorm on ways that you can help each other.

Getting involved in social activities is another form of networking. Meetup.com is a site that posts social networking events nationwide on all kinds of topics. If you are a trekkie, a baseball fan, a movie buff, a real estate mogul, or a scuba diver, you can attend an event in your neighborhood with other like-minded people. You may not talk about your job search during the first conversation like you do at an in-transition group, but trust me, the topic will eventually come up as you get to know your backgammon partner, your scrabble buddy or your fellow astrology reader.

Volunteering is a form of networking also. As you are building the Habitat for Humanity house, feeding the homeless or helping to design the neighborhood haunted house, you will find many ways to get to know the people around you. Take advantage of all these opportunities to make new friends and to be open to new possibilities.

> *Absolutely Abby's Advice:* *Networking is the art of building relationships, which as you know, is an important skill to master in any job. Networking is not about you asking everyone you know for help. It's about "paying it forward" and asking how you can help them first. You have been networking long before you knew you were doing it, and you should continue to do it long after you land. Cultivate your relationships so that they grow into lifelong friendships — that is the true meaning of networking.*

▪ 55 ▪ Lessons from Our Feathered Friends

"Lessons From Geese" was transcribed from a speech given by Angeles Arrien at the 1991 Organizational Development Network and was based on the work of Milton Olson. Not only can we learn about searching from the geese, we can also learn how to behave once we land.

FACT: As each goose flaps its wings it creates an "uplift" for the birds that follow. By flying in a "V" formation, the whole flock adds 71% greater flying range than if each bird flew alone. When a goose falls out of formation, it suddenly feels the drag and resistance of flying alone. It quickly moves back into formation to take advantage of the lifting power of the bird immediately in front of it.

> LESSON: People who share a common direction and sense of community can get where they are going quicker and easier because they are traveling on the thrust of one another. If we have as much sense as a goose, we stay in formation with those headed where we want to go. We are willing to accept their help and give our help to others.

>> *Abby says: This is why networking is so important – by helping your fellow jobseekers, your ride will be easier. Once you land, teamwork is critical for on the job success.*

FACT: When the lead goose tires, it rotates back into formation and another goose flies to the point position.

> LESSON: It pays to take turns doing the hard tasks and sharing leadership. As with geese, people are interdependent on each other's skills, capabilities and unique arrangements of gifts, talents or resources.

>> *Abby says: Find a job search buddy who is searching for a similar role in a similar industry. Do not be concerned about competing. Two heads are often better than one. Compensate for each other's weaknesses and you will get past the challenging times together.*

FACT: The geese flying in formation honk to encourage those up front to keep up their speed.

LESSON: We need to make sure our honking is encouraging. In groups where there is encouragement, the production is much greater. The power of encouragement (to stand by one's heart or core values and encourage the heart and core of others) is the quality of honking we seek.

> *Abby says: Join a networking group for some old fashioned honking. If you don't find honking when you get there, join a different group. Spend the most time with the friends and family who honk the loudest.*

FACT: When a goose gets sick, wounded or shot down, two geese drop out of formation and follow it to help and protect it. They stay with it until it dies or is able to fly again. Then, they launch out with another formation or catch up with the flock.

> LESSON: If we have as much sense as geese, we will stand by each other in difficult times as well as when we are strong.

> *Abby says: No matter how badly you feel right now, you can always find someone who is in worse shape than you. Find that person and help them find their way the way that others have guided you.*

Absolutely Abby's Advice: *There are lessons to be learned from everything – you just have to open your eyes to see them. The next time that you see a flock of geese, think about whether you have learned their lesson. Are you helping enough people or are you just asking for help? Make it a goal to help someone with something every day, even if it's your child with her homework. You'll be glad you did.*

▪ 56 ▪ The 7 Deadly Sins of Networking

While many of us strive for perfection in our job search and in our networking, we occasionally fall short of perfection. The key is to learn where changes can be made quickly to improve our odds of success. I hereby offer you the 7 Deadly Sins of Networking:

1) Do not go to a networking event with a negative attitude. Instead, put on a smile and think positively about all the wonderful opportunities that could be in store for you. If you've had a bad day, you might want to call a friend for some good old fashioned cheering up before heading to the event.

2) Don't have a "what can you do for me attitude". Building a network requires helping others first so they'll feel good about helping you. Do not expect someone to offer you a job or even an interview. Instead, expect that you will make some great connections, which may lead you to other connections, and so on, until you find that lead that lands you a job.

3) Do not forget to bring business cards. Do not bring stained cards or folded cards. Business cards are just one of the many ways that you make an impression on other people. Do not make the event just about handing out business cards. Don't hand someone your business card until after you've taken the time to get to know at least a little bit about him or her.

4) Do not assume that just going to an event is networking, because 90% of networking is what happens AFTER the event is over. Schedule individual appointments for coffee so you can learn more about the people whom you felt a common connection with.

5) If you use LinkedIn to network and you ask to be introduced, don't ask to be "recommended" if you don't know the person

referring you. Rather, ask for a "referral". When asking for referrals, don't ask the same people to help you all the time. Keep networking so that you have more people who you can ask for referrals.

6) Do not tell someone you are going to follow up if you're not planning to. As soon as you can, write the action you agreed to take on the back of his/her business card. Develop the habit of doing all your follow-up within 24 hours of the event – any longer and it's easy to forget what you've learned about your connections.

And the worst sin of them all...

7) Do not network ONLY when you are searching for a job. You should be keeping your network current all year round. Join networking groups in your field or industry to keep up with the news in your professional community.

> *Absolutely Abby's Advice:* *The good thing about these sins is that they are not all that deadly, and you can ultimately be forgiven if you change your ways. The first way to repent is to start "paying it forward". Call old networking contacts you have lost touch with and ask them how they are, followed by a question on how you can help them achieve their goals. Helping others be successful is the first major step towards forming a strong, lifelong network.*

▪ 57 ▪ Networking is Not Just For Not Working

As I look back on the past few years attending in-transition groups, I think of all the wonderful lessons I have learned about networking. These are lessons that you can't learn in a book or a classroom... you have to experience them for yourself.

Although these lessons may seem basic, they are extremely powerful:

Help everyone you can, even if you don't think you have the time to

Each time that you help someone, you are changing their world, and in some cases, you are changing their world drastically for the better. If you give them one interviewing tip that helps them land the job of their dreams, you have changed their life. Happy people tend to be more willing to help more people. If everyone in the world starting helping each other, can you imagine how much richer our world might be? I can.

Become a "Norm"

If you remember the TV show "Cheers", the character Norm was well known to everyone at Sam's. When he walked in the room, everyone would yell, "Norm!" When you consistently attend your favorite networking group, people will start to remember you, and it will be easier for them to remember to send opportunities your way. Popularity is very contagious, as you will learn.

Become a resource for your networking group

Everyone is an expert at something. Determine what you are good at and then share it with the world. Bring your expertise to your networking group and teach people about what you know. Becoming a resource turns you into a leader and leaders tend to climb the corporate ladder more rapidly. Spread your wings and try leadership on for size. If your group already has a leader, offer to assist with membership or with program planning. Leaders always need help and if they lead by example, you may have found yourself a mentor. Then, when you're ready… step up to the plate and start swinging. You may even decide to form your own group some day.

<u>Networking is not Just for Not Working</u>

Everyone at every age has challenges. They can be health related, money related, school related, relationship related, job related, etc. I used to think that going to a networking event was about job searching. As my friend Jerome Laday says so eloquently, "Networking is not Just for Not Working". I have learned over the past few years that networking is about friendships. Sharing your challenges with other people makes you realize how much you have in common. You don't have to share them with the entire group, but you may want to develop a small group of networking friends to confide in. Sharing enhances relationships and improves the feeling of community within the group. Everyone needs help sometime with something. Be willing to share and be willing to help.

> ***Absolutely Abby's Advice:*** *The lessons that I learned while networking have not only changed the focus of my career but also the focus of my life. Networking can be an outlet for you to share, to celebrate, and to help people with their challenges. Give true networking a try. Your investment will come back in droves.*

▪ 58 ▪ Hitting Your Jackpot

On a recent trip to Las Vegas, I started to wonder about why some people seem to be luckier in life than others, especially when it comes to meeting the right people at the right time. Are they luck or are they simply practicing the "Never Ending Interview"?

When you are searching for a job (and even when you're not), you are being evaluated during every conversation that you have. The problem is that you never know which conversations are interviews in disguise and which ones are just friendly banter. Therefore, you always need to be on your toes – just in case. I call this "The Never Ending Interview".

When it comes to job searching, you need lots of skill, lots of ingenuity and a little bit of luck. But is it really luck, or is it about always being prepared for an interview that comes into play?

Consider an aspiring actress who is working as a waitress in New York City until she lands her next role. If the producer of a new Broadway show happens to get hungry at the exact time that the waitress' table is ready for more patrons, is that luck?

What about the conductor who is jolly every morning despite the train delays and the rainy weather? If a sales manager is searching for customer service representatives and asks the conductor to stop by his office to fill out an application, is that luck?

Or how about a grocery store clerk who takes extra special care of her customers? What if the customer checking out was searching for a new receptionist for her office and invited the clerk in for an interview? Is that luck?

Better yet, think about a computer technician who attends a new networking event and happens to sit at a table next to an unemployed CIO. If the CIO gets hired a week later and then offers the technician a position, is that luck?

So is there a way to improve your "luck" or are some people just naturally luckier than others? As the saying goes, you have to be in it to win it. Staying at home all day and applying for positions online reduces the opportunities for serendipitous occurrences. Being at the right place at the right time can only happen if you start with being at the right place.

How do you know what the "right place" is? You don't. That's the fun of the Never Ending Interview. The more that you put yourself out there, the more chance you have to be "lucky".

> ***Absolutely Abby's Advice:*** *Perhaps you believe that your "luck" is really good karma, destiny, positive thinking, prayers being answered, just being in the right place at the right time, or the Law of Attraction, but whatever it is, a dose of "luck" certainly comes in handy.*

▪ 59 ▪ The Painting Paralegal & Soccer Practice

Here is a great example of the Never Ending Interview in action, when someone was in the right place at the right time. An attorney friend of mine, who I'll call John, was searching for a new apartment for his family in New York City. Anyone who has ever hunted for an affordable yet spacious apartment in Manhattan knows that it can be just as daunting as searching for a job in a down economy. It takes creativity, flexibility, and lots of patience.

One day, as John was searching on the web, a new apartment listing popped up. He immediately scheduled an appointment for that same day so that he wouldn't miss out on the opportunity. John arrived at the apartment 15 minutes ahead of schedule and saw a young woman spraying fresh paint on the walls. In speaking with her, John discovered that she was recently downsized from a law firm where she was working as a paralegal. As it happened, John's law firm was going through an expansion and was searching for a paralegal. Within a week, the painter was hired, all because she was professional, articulate, and personable.

When John told me this story, he also mentioned that in the past he had hired waiters, supermarket clerks, and people who operated rides at amusement parks. He told me that when he meets people with strong communication skills and a dynamic personality, he hands them his business card and asks them to send him their resume. When a position opens up at his law firm, he digs through his e-mails to find these candidates to see if he can make a match.

Another friend of mine, a fellow recruiter, tells a story about how he landed a job because of a chat he had while watching his son play soccer. While speaking with a fellow parent on the bleachers, he discovered that the parent was the owner of a technology recruiting firm in New Jersey. Lo and behold, the owner was searching for a new recruiter to add to his team, and my friend had been searching for weeks. He was hired three days later.

When you're in the job market, do not be ashamed to tell everyone that you come into contact what you are looking for. You can even tell the person next to you on line at the mall that you are looking. But, beware! Refrain from being pushy or having a "woe is me attitude" when you tell them, because they will be less likely to want to help you. But, with a well-crafted elevator pitch you can find many people who are willing to at least brainstorm with you and give you some ideas to try that you may not have thought of.

> **Absolutely Abby's Advice:** *The next time you're bored on line at the supermarket, try chatting with your also-bored line buddy rather than listening to your iPod or reading a magazine. Your new supermarket buddy may become your new boss, your new co-worker, or if nothing else, your new best friend.*

▪ 60 ▪ Trash Talking Your Way to a Job

The Never Ending Interview happens when you least expect it.

Did you ever think that taking out the trash could help you with your job search? Well apparently it once did. Someone from an online networking group that I belong to posted this:

"NEVER underestimate the power of networking, even when you are throwing out the trash. That's how I found out about what turned out to be one of the best jobs in my career. I was at the trash dump in my condo complex and greeted a new homeowner. Next thing I know I have an interview, and an offer, at the company where she worked."

When you are in job search mode, you are always on an interview and should act accordingly, even at the trashcan. In her post, this person said that when she arrived at the trashcans, she greeted the new homeowner. I'm sure that she did more than greet her. Rather than acting like Oscar the Grouch, I'm sure she asked friendly "getting to know you" questions that ultimately revealed the opportunity before her.

Your parents were somewhat incorrect when they taught you not to talk to strangers. They should have said, "Once you become an adult, talk to strangers and offer to help them." Strangers are everywhere. They are on the long lines at the store. They are the neighbors you haven't had the nerve to introduce yourself to yet. They are your bartenders and waiters. They are the people dressed up like goblins at your Halloween party. And, they don't have to be strangers forever, as some of them might even turn into friends.

> *Absolutely Abby's Advice:* *Take advantage of every opportunity you have to start friendly conversations with strangers. You never know which one of them might actually have a job opportunity for you, or might pass you to their friend who does. Begin your conversations by offering to help in whatever way you can. One day that stranger may just take you by the hand and lead you to the finish line.*

▪ 61 ▪ Becoming a Pop Star or Marketing Star

Here are two more stories based on the Never Ending Interview.

My friend Liz, a senior pharmaceutical marketing manager, was informed that her job was going to be eliminated within three months due to budget cuts. Having been through this before, Liz knew that she had to do things differently than everyone else. She knew that there had to be a few start-up pharmaceutical companies who might consider hiring her as a marketing consultant while she searched for more permanent opportunities. She sent out several introductory letters to Vice Presidents of Marketing hoping to hear some good news. One day she discovered that her former manager from 15 years ago was the owner of a company that was about to launch a new product. Rather than risking snail mail delays, Liz called the owner to congratulate him on his new company's success and he asked her to join him for lunch to reminisce about the old days. Over a chef's salad, Liz's former boss offered her a job as his new Vice President of Marketing, a job that was not even on his radar yet to fill. It only took one phone call and some outside-the box thinking. Seem far-fetched? Liz would have thought the same thing.

The Never Ending Interview even works for celebrities. One day, talk show host Ellen DeGeneres, was interviewing Mandy Moore, the pop star from the 90's, about her new album. As Mandy described how she had been "discovered", I listened and realized it was an example of yet another Never Ending Interview opportunity. Mandy was 14 at the time and she was recording a song at a studio. A Fed Ex delivery man came in to pick up a package and starting chatting with Mandy. She mentioned that she was recording a song and hoped to send a demo out soon. The Fed Ex man told her that he knew someone who knew someone who knew someone who was a Vice President at Epic Records and asked if she wanted him to send the demo in for her. The rest is history…Mandy became a star and Mr. Fed Ex quit his job and became a talent scout.

> **Absolutely Abby's Advice:** *Wherever and whenever you're out and about, remember the Never Ending Interview. You never know who may be lurking around the corner who can help you become a star.*

▪ 62 ▪ Flexibility For Success

According to the Wiktionary, the word "flexible" is defined as "willing or ready to yield to the influence of others; not invincibly rigid or obstinate; tractable; manageable; easy and compliant." According to Absolutely Abby, being flexible will score you all sorts of points with recruiters and hiring managers, but being too flexible may cause you trouble down the road.

Is this market, employers are looking for people who can quickly adapt to the changing times and to their changing organization. Here are some ways to demonstrate your flexibility to an employer:

1) Most recruiters and hiring managers prefer to schedule in-person interviews during the normal workday, i.e., between 9 and 5. Make every attempt to work within those confines so as not to inconvenience the people whose approval is essential for your success.

2) When you get to the interview, expect that there will be delays and/or cancellations, especially if you are going to be meeting with multiple people on one day. Expecting that your interviews will start and end on time will cause you to be unnecessarily frustrated and aggravated. Pacing around the reception area will not bode well for you. Bring some industry related materials to read while you wait and perhaps discuss what you read with your interviewer.

3) Expect that you may be required to interview with as many as five or six people before you are offered a position. When the call comes asking you to return to the company for a 7th time, accept happily and thank the company for inviting you back.

113

While it is important to demonstrate your flexibility, there are times when being too flexible can be to your detriment. Here are some examples:

1) If your target company only offers two weeks of vacation for the next five years, consider whether you will really be happy working for them. For those of you who enjoy your time off, this may not be the best job for you.

2) If you don't feel that the job description is at least 75% interesting to you, you may want to wait for a better match. Not loving your job or worse yet, being bored with it, may cause you to want to start looking again within the year, and that won't be much fun.

3) We all have a "little voice" in our heads that helps us decide what is right for us and what isn't. If your little voice tells you that you don't have chemistry with your prospective boss, or that you don't like the people who will be on your team, or that the company culture doesn't fit with your preferences, you should definitely listen to the voice. Making a bad choice is worse than choosing wrong. You have much less time to look for a job when you're working in the wrong job. Take the time now to find the RIGHT job, not just A job.

> *Absolutely Abby's Advice:* *Create a list of the components you're looking for in a new job, in a new company, and in a new boss. Review that list before every interview to determine if the position meets a majority of your requirements. Then, proceed full speed ahead while being a flexible candidate along the way. Follow these steps and everyone will win, especially you!*

▪ 63 ▪ Be Available

A jobseeker I met at a networking event was venting about the frustration she was feeling while actively trying to connect with a recruiter. She said that a recruiter had left her a message just as she was leaving on vacation. When she returned from vacation she could not reach the recruiter again. With all the competition vying for airtime, I was not the least bit surprised.

Back in 1994 when Gloria Estefan was the hottest ticket in town and I started my recruiting career, life was different. For one thing, I had no gray hair. For another, when I applied for 15 jobs, at least half of the recruiters at the companies were interested in speaking with me. They would leave me a message on my now dead and buried answering machine, and I would return it the next day only to have them jump for joy as they answered their ringing phone. That was then, but this is now.

Now when a company runs an ad, they receive hundreds if not thousands of resumes. With the advent of "click here to apply" job boards, you no longer have to stuff and lick envelopes, go to Kinko's to fax resumes, or buy stamps from Mr. Mailman. If it's so easy for you to click, think of how easy it is for your competition to click.

When you do manage to connect with a recruiter, express your Absolute delight as soon as you can. Then muster all of the passion that you have and continue the phone screen. Speak with the recruiter while smiling into a mirror or walk around the house to keep your energy at its maximum level. The recruiters who appreciate your effort and believe in your skills will then be happy to invite you in for a live interview.

> **Absolutely Abby's Advice:** *If you are in job search mode, be available 24/7 to answer your phone. Make sure that 3-year-old Joey or your cousin who is visiting from another country is not the one answering your cell phone. If you are planning to go on vacation, take your phone with you to the beach. Recruiters who don't find you are going to hang up and try someone else. Be the someone else that they find when your competition misses their call. Regardless of the job market you can't afford to be MIA.*

▪ 64 ▪ Practice Makes Perfect

We've all heard the expression that practice makes perfect. That expression could not be more correct when it comes to interviewing.

A first interview is very similar to a first date. Two people are evaluating whether they should take their relationship to the next level or end it once and for all. Both events cause anxiety about what to say, what to wear, and how to act. When you are dating, you practice over and over again. So shouldn't you practice interviewing too? Absolutely!

A mock interview is simply a practice interview. But, as with any training regiment, you have to step slightly out of your comfort zone in order to improve. Your mock interviewer can be a friend, a family member, or a professional such as a career coach. A career coach is ideal for many reasons. For one, they won't hesitate to gently and honestly tell you what you might need to improve. These professionals are also much more likely to notice things about you that your friends or family might not.

Start by preparing a list of questions for your mock interviewer to ask you. You might begin by listing some of the questions you've been asked in actual interviews that made you sweat. Then add some new questions to the list to keep the mock interview interesting. There are many books with sample interview questions, so preparing a long list should be easy.

Ask your mock interviewer to not only evaluate your words, but also your body language, as most of what you communicate during interviews is non-verbal. Remind them to point out those pesky little habits that you have (hair twirling, frowning, leaning on a chair arm, tapping your fingernails), as these can be deal breakers. Relish the feedback on all the less than perfect things you said or did that could render you offer-less.

For an extra challenge, schedule yourself for a follow-up mock interview in a setting that seems realistic. Meet your mock interviewer at his/her office after hours, or in a hotel lobby or coffee shop. Perhaps you'll make this a dress rehearsal as well and arrive in your freshly pressed interview suit.

> **Absolutely Abby's Advice:** *While laughter is the best medicine, I recommend that you ask your interviewer to keep the mockery to a minimum to ensure success. And, then practice, practice, practice. You have no idea how much more comfortable you will feel when it's your turn for the spotlight.*

▪ 65 ▪ Don't Let Your Dog Eat Your Homework

Although when you are unemployed you may believe that any job will do, I am here to tell you that thinking that way may lead to more trouble for you than you deserve. The last thing that you want to be doing a year after you start your new job is searching for a new one because you made a hasty decision without doing your homework. To avoid these missteps, pretend you are a journalist writing an article about the company you are interviewing with. Do the research beforehand, and then ask questions during the interview to complete the story.

In the days of yore, we learned about companies from the library, the newspaper or from their annual report. Now that we have access to the Internet, the world is rich with vast amounts of information to be devoured. These are the top things to look for when researching a company before your interview:

1) Review the company's website from head to toe at a basic level. Look at their media section. Read the most current press releases and any others that can help you learn about the health of the company. Prepare some questions about the things that you learn.

2) Search for your interviewer on Google and LinkedIn. Learn about their background, where they graduated from, what their hobbies are, etc. See if you have anything in common that can help you develop instant rapport.

3) If the company is a public company, look at the stock price and notice whether it is trending up or down. Prepare related observations and questions for the interview.

4) Look at the career page if there is one. Notice the number of open jobs, the types of jobs, and the levels. This may tell you the story about the company's turnover.

5) Look at the company's benefits section. If the topic comes up during the interview, you'll be able to ask for more detailed information beyond the basics.

If you have done all of this homework, I guarantee that you will develop more intelligent questions than "What is the dress code?" or "What are the core hours?" or "How many vacation days do I get?" Well thought out questions show your interviewer that you are carefully considering their job and not simply shopping for the best compensation and benefits package.

Here are some questions you might ask based on your research:

1) What are the company's strengths and weaknesses compared to its competition?

2) How important does upper management consider the function of this department/position?

3) What is the organization's plan for the next five years, and how does this department fit in?

> **Absolutely Abby's Advice:** *Doing your homework before an interview is an essential part of your success. Knowing detailed information about the company will not only help you ask the right questions, but it will also help you understand if this is the ideal company for you to spend the next several years at. Most importantly, showing that you have done your homework demonstrates that you are truly interested in the company and its products, which ultimately will make companies more eager to have you on their team.*

▪ 66 ▪ The Proof is in the Portfolio

Think of your resume as your marketing collateral and your interview as your marketing pitch. In a similar vein, a portfolio is the perfect vehicle to help demonstrate that you can actually do what your resume says you have done. It is a great way to complete your marketing package.

Your portfolio becomes a history of your professional life, which evolves as you evolve. It should provide a glimpse of who you are as a potential employee and should present a professional image encapsulated in a leather binder.

Avoid putting information in your portfolio that a former company would deem confidential and inappropriate for external viewing. Stick with items that are neutral or related to you personally. Here are some documents to add to your portfolio:

✓ Awards or honors – other than your "cleanest bunk" award from band camp, choose awards and honors that continue to remain relevant over time

✓ Performance appraisals – only if they are positive overall and do not divulge many weaknesses

✓ Transcripts – assuming that you were strong academically and that your major is relevant to your current career

✓ Congratulatory e-mails and recommendations – notes from peers or superiors commending you on your work

✓ Samples of your work that you have permission to share – research papers, lab work, charts and graphs, proposals, writing samples, presentations, flyers, websites, etc.

✓ Agendas of meetings or workshops you designed and/or implemented

✓ Certificates of attendance at seminars or workshops

✓ Photographs of professional occasions – keep these to a minimum and be sure they are relevant

✓ Copies of professional licenses and certificates

✓ Copies of your resume – in case you forget to bring one to the interview

Creating sections with titles on them will help you quickly flip to the most relevant information for the particular interview. Some interviewers will prefer to quickly thumb through the book themselves while others will ask you to choose some a few documents to explain in detail.

Typically, hiring managers are more interested in seeing your portfolio than Human Resources professionals and recruiters are. Wait until at least half of the interview time has gone by and then, ask your interviewer if they would like to see some samples of your work, rather than assuming that they are automatically interested. Interviewers who learn visually will probably appreciate your documents more than those who are auditory learners.

> *Absolutely Abby's Advice:* *A portfolio is a great way to make a lasting impression and also distinguish yourself from your competitors for coveted open jobs. The proof is in the pudding but it can also be in your portfolio. Just try to avoid spilling pudding on it before the interview.*

▪ 67 ▪ Suit-able Interviews

Several years ago, I was searching for an Executive Assistant who, when hired, would report to the CFO of the Fortune 500 firm I was working for. I received hundreds of resumes and was pleased to receive several candidates that seemed qualified. Then, one jumped right out of the pile – I'll call that candidate Betty.

Betty wrote a creative cover letter explaining why she was the perfect candidate. She dotted her i's and crossed her t's, and had a mastery of the English language. The words on the page made me believe that she was not only someone I wanted to interview, but also that she was probably the person we would ultimately hire. My intuition rarely lets me down, or so I thought.

I called Betty on the phone and, lo and behold, her phone presence was just as wonderful as her resume and cover letter. I could not wait to meet her, so I scheduled an interview for the next day. I even asked the CFO to clear a half hour on his calendar because I was sure that I had found his next Executive Assistant.

121

In walked Betty. She greeted our receptionist warmly, took her seat, and patiently waited for me. I got up from my desk and started the walk to the waiting area while thinking about how happy the CFO would be with me after he met Betty. What a lucky day for everyone involved!

But then it all went wrong…

Betty broke the cardinal sin of interviewing. She neglected to dress to impress. Although the outfit she was wearing was attractive, it was not nearly corporate enough for an Executive Assistant to the CFO. On a positive note, it would have been the perfect outfit for the company holiday party.

I began the interview with Betty but my excitement waned, as I was concerned about her judgment. If Betty wasn't able to make the right choice with this level of decision, how could she possibly make more important decisions on behalf of the CFO? Also, what would she wear to work every day if this was her best outfit? I decided to pass on Betty and moved on to additional candidates.

> **Absolutely Abby's Advice:** *It is Absolutely essential that you dress professionally for your interviews. You do not need to have the most expensive suit in order to impress a recruiter. A clean, pressed, and well-fitting suit from a discount clothing store will suffice. Never assume that because the company has a casual or business casual dress code that you should dress that way for your interview. Dressing to impress will help you make an excellent first impression, and will ensure that your foot is firmly inserted in the door.*

▪ 68 ▪ A Breath of Fresh Air

Back in the days of yore when I was interviewing candidates galore, I interviewed one particular applicant who left a strong impression on me...

I was searching for an accountant and finally had the ideal candidate's resume lying on my desk, let's call him John. All I needed was to meet him and the score would be 1-0 in my favor. When I went out to greet John in the lobby, I quickly learned something about him within the first three seconds – it was apparent that he had eaten onions for lunch. Throughout the interview it was hard to concentrate on John's words as I kept being reminded of his recent meal. If only I would have kept the noseplugs I wore when I first learned to swim in my desk, as they would have come in handy.

As much as your words and body language are being evaluated during an interview, your professional appearance and hygiene is also on display and must be in tip-top shape. If this was a once-in-a-career event I wouldn't bother mentioning this to you, but this seemingly small error has crinkled my nose time and time again. Always, always, always, carry mints or gum in your pocket, especially when you are in job search mode. Five minutes before you expect to start talking to anyone, including the receptionist, pop one of them into your mouth (and finish it before you start talking). Here are some reminders on other things you can do to be sure you are making a good first impression.

1) Be sure to check your clothes for holes, dirt, wrinkles, and stains before you put them on, and remember to shine your shoes.

2) Women's nails do not have to be manicured but if they are, choose a pastel color. Your interviewer should be focused on you, and not on your fingernails. Women and men, make sure that you have clean fingernails as well.

3) You can certainly wear jewelry but it should not be flashy. Leave your tongue rings at home unless you would only consider working for companies that permit you to wear one on the job. Also leave your baseball cap and sun glasses at home.

4) Your hair should be neat and professional. Women who choose to wear makeup should be sure that it's subtle and unassuming. Also, do not go overboard on the perfume or cologne – your interviewer may be overwhelmed by it, or worse, allergic to it.

5) Carrying a nice briefcase portrays a much more professional image to your interviewer or networking buddy, and it can also be a nice confidence booster for you. Remember to clean out all of the piles of papers from your last few interviews so that you appear to be organized.

> *Absolutely Abby's Advice: Top-notch interview skills and a strong resume are absolute requirements for a successful job search. As important as it is to prep for your interview by dotting your i's and crossing your t's on your resume, it is critical that you devote the same amount of time to perfecting your professional appearance. Once you do that, you will be a breath of fresh air!*

▪ 69 ▪ Good Timing Is Key

Patience is a virtue – and you need to have plenty of it on the day of your interview.

One of the worst things that can happen to you on your big day is to be late for your interview. It will add a heightened level of stress to your already anxious state. Always try to arrive to the interview *at least 30 minutes* before it starts. For those of you who believe time is infinite, aim for an hour before.

If you're driving, take a dry run the night before to make sure that your GPS won't get you lost (blaming your GPS works a lot better than blaming yourself). If you're train-ing or bus-ing or boat-ing or ferry-ing, add a bunch of extra time for the passenger, who will undoubtedly choose the day of your interview to get sick. You can thank Murphy and his Law for that.

If you arrive early as planned, grab a bottle of water at a local eatery. This gives you some time to catch your breath and also to freshen your breath, the latter being way more important to your interviewer. And, you can also visit the restroom to make sure that you didn't miss a button, that there are no annoying pieces of hair out of place, and that there is no cat fur on your leg. Why do they insist on wishing you luck on your interview by rubbing up against you just as you are walking out the door?

If traffic is light on the day of your interview you'll have even more extra time to spare. Take a short trip around the neighborhood to see what kinds of venues you'll be able to visit during your lunch break once you land the job. Or, find a local bookstore and browse your favorite magazines. Choose G-rated ones in case your interviewer happens to be standing next to you.

> ***Absolutely Abby's Advice:*** *Do not…and I repeat…DO NOT check in more than 15 minutes early for your interview. Your recruiter will become discombobulated, which is not helpful for anyone. Instead, remember that patience is a virtue. Then, muster all the confidence and the fresh breath that you have, and go on in.*

Ingenious Interviews

▪ 70 ▪ Interview Nerves Be Gone!

If you think that standard one-on-one interviews are the most intimidating thing on the planet, you clearly have not yet experienced the videoconference or the group interview.

Back in 1997, I interviewed for a recruiting position for a company that produced major sporting events. Because the hiring manager was in a faraway land, the interview took place via videoconference. Talk about intimidating! Back then, there was a delay in the conversation so when I said "one of my greatest strengths is managing large expansions", the interviewer just sat and stared awkwardly at me until he heard my answer. Since then, the technology has improved, so time delays are no longer a problem. However, these types of interviews can still be distracting. Try to ignore how strange it is to watch yourself on the preview screen. Don't be concerned with what might look like a stain on your shirt or food in your teeth. Instead, try to focus on how you sound, rather than on how you look.

Another kind of interview, which is growing in popularity, is the group or panel interview. On the surface, it feels like an unfair battle – 3-5 people against one, where each person appears to be waiting for you to say something silly. Just think of it this way – the great part about a group interview is that it saves you lots of time – you get to interview once instead of five times, which means that you'll have four fewer chances to say something less than perfect. And, you won't have to remember to give consistent answers to everyone. If the group is prepared, they will have already divided up the questions among the interviewers. Typically the interviewers will speak with you one at a time. This feels like you are having a one-on-one conversation with four other people gawking. Not as much of a big deal if you think about it that way, right? If it still seems intimidating, imagine your interviewers each in their underwear like

127

Marcia Brady from "The Brady Bunch" did during her driving test. Just don't burst out laughing.

> **Absolutely Abby's Advice:** *Whether it's a group interview, a videoconference or an old-fashioned interview, remind yourself that you are actually the one doing the evaluating. That is, you are interviewing the company to determine if you want to pour your blood, sweat, and tears into their products and services for the next 3-5 years. Do not take this choice lightly. Choosing the wrong job is far worse than staying unemployed – I need not remind you of the many reasons why. So go into your interviews with confidence and credibility and then determine which companies are worthy of your talents. Your future depends on it!*

▪ 71 ▪   The Language of Body Language

Many people underestimate the importance of body language during the interview process. Based on your body language, an interviewer will make assumptions about whether or not you are self-assured, energetic, timid, truthful, stress prone, nice, enthusiastic, funny, etc.

The truth of the matter is that your body language actually speaks louder than your words do. Studies show that when we are communicating, only 7% of the information received is verbal or the words that we use to get our point across. Our vocal communication consists of pitch, speed, volume and tone of voice, representing only 38% of the communicated information. The 55% that remains to be judged during an interview is our body language.

Two of the most vital parts of body language are your hands and arms.

If you have a faulty internal temperature control device like me, you typically find it difficult to warm up regardless of the season. One of the most common things we do, when we are beginning to feel chilly, is to fold our arms around ourselves to keep warm. This is a big no-no in an interview and should be avoided at all costs, even if your lips are turning blue, which mine frequently are. Crossing your arms makes you appear insecure, uncomfortable, defensive, or closed minded, none of which will be received positively during an interview.

Let your hands lie loosely on your lap, or place them on the armrests of the chair until you need to use them. Keeping your hands stiffly by your side or stuck in your pockets can give the impression that you're insecure and uncomfortable.

Use hand gestures (the clean kind) to liven up the interview and to make you appear to be at ease. Don't start with too many at first but add them slowly as you go along. Your gestures will eventually seem natural to you so that you do not have to think about them.

The gesture that is most often underestimated in importance is the handshake. No one wants to shake hands with a clammy or droopy hand, as it resembles shaking hands with a fish (not that I've tried this before). No matter what the circumstance is, a dry, firm (but not painful), handshake should do the trick. This indicates strength, power and confidence.

> **Absolutely Abby's Advice:** *The hands and arms can be powerful additions to your interviewing toolbox if you know how to use them. They can help you get your point across to your interviewer in subtle ways that even he or she may not be aware of. Give yourself a helping hand by studying your body language before, during and after an interview. You may learn remarkable things about yourself that can dramatically improve your rate of interviewing success.*

▪ 72 ▪ The Best Seat in the House

Similar to your hand gestures, your position at the table and also in your seat can also affect your rate of success.

When you walk into the interview room, you are typically motioned towards a specific seat. In most cases the room only has two chairs and unless you haven't eaten your Wheaties that day, you are quite aware of which one should be yours. However, in the cases when you are escorted to a conference room with several chairs, choose a seat that is caddy-cornered to the recruiter. Typically friends or colleagues sit closer to each other than interviewer and interviewee, so this chair position suggests that you are "on the same team".

During the interview, lean somewhat forward to show an interest in what the other person is saying. But, avoid leaning too far forward and seeming awkwardly eager. By contrast, tipping back in the chair is a sign of overconfidence and projects arrogance. You also want to avoid tipping over, which would be a great story for your friends but a bad story for your interview. Finally, another pose to avoid is the leg cross with one ankle rested on the knee as it conveys an overly casual attitude.

Your posture reflects your energy, enthusiasm and self-control. The goal is to adopt a posture that demonstrates interest and confidence, but also relaxation. Sit up straight in your chair with your back against the rear of the chair. If you slouch or hang sideways in your chair, it leaves the impression that you are not that interested in the job or that you are lethargic or lackadaisical. Sitting on the edge of your chair gives the appearance of tension and or uncomfortable feelings.

> **Absolutely Abby's Advice:** *The key is to find a position and stick with it. Constant shifting can make you look...well..."shifty". Be glad that you have earned a seat at the table, and then sit tight and hang on for the ride!*

▪ 73 ▪ Mirroring Without Mimicking

Assuming you are qualified for the job, getting a "yes" vote depends on whether or not the interviewer finds you engaging, and feels comfortable with you. Besides using words to develop rapport, you also may find success using a technique called "mirroring".

People generally like people who are similar to them, and believe me, you want your interviewer to like you. Therefore, by observing an interviewer's body language and reflecting this back at him by subtly mirroring his movements, he is likely to feel more at ease and friendly towards you.

Here are three ways to mirror your interviewer:

1) Pay close attention to your interviewer's gestures. If he often uses his hands while explaining things to you, try to do this as well. If he doesn't use many gestures, keep yours to a minimum.

2) Notice his body posture and adopt a similar one. If he is sitting up straight and tall, you should do the same. If he leans forward, mirror his actions several minutes later.

3) Notice the speed at which your interviewer speaks and adapt your own pace to his. Match his style including tone, rhythm, and pronunciation. If you do this, you will score points that you didn't even know were up for grabs.

While you are mirroring behaviors, you don't want to appear to be mimicking because it feels like mocking. For example, just remember a time when little Johnny starting repeating everything you said, word for word, just to annoy you. Practicing the mirroring skill will help it become second nature to you and less obvious to the interviewer.

Here are two kinds of body language to look out for from your interviewer:

1) If you notice your interviewer lean backwards in her chair, lean forwards in yours several minutes later, so as not to be too obvious. Leaning forward should draw her back into the conversation.

2) If the interviewer shakes his head or sighs or crosses his arms, consider this to be an obvious sign of displeasure. Assume that you need to win back some points, and quickly.

> **Absolutely Abby's Advice:** *Like everything else about interviewing, effective mirroring requires polish and precision. Practicing this skill, while also learning how to best explain your strengths to an interviewer, will help you soar to success in the interviewing game.*

▪ 74 ▪ The 4 C's of Interviewing

Instead of thinking of an interview as a person asking questions and trying to stump you, think of it as a two-way conversation.

In kindergarten, we learned that when other people are speaking, we need to listen or we will be asked to sit in the corner. So many times I have wished that there was a corner in my office to send people to. When an interviewer asks you a question, make sure that you answer it by following the 4 C's of Interviewing:

1) Be Calm – During every interview, regardless of how prepared you are, someone is going to ask you a stumper. Sometimes the stumpers are used just to see how you react to difficult situations. And sometimes, there isn't even a right answer. When a stumper comes along, take a deep breath and put on your thinking cap. Ask for some time to reflect or ask the interviewer to repeat or rephrase the question. If you are really stumped, ask if you can come back to the question later, like when you were taking your

SAT. Then remain calm, take your best guess and focus your positive energy and attention on the next set of questions.

2) Be Clear – Many people find it difficult to explain what their strengths and accomplishments really are. As difficult as it is, you MUST learn to develop the skill to successfully convey what you bring to the table. Practice describing and then memorize your accomplishments in the form of SAR's – Situations, Actions, and Results. Then, offer the interviewer the most appropriate SAR when the question is asked.

3) Be Convincing – To be convincing, you have to first believe in yourself. You have to believe that you are the best person to fill the position and that the position is the perfect match for your personality, interests and skills. If you don't honestly believe one or the other, there is no way that you be will able to convince the interviewer that you are the best person for the job. But, on the other hand, if you know that this is the right company, the right industry, and the right job for you, don't be shy about it. Let your interviewer know. Enthusiastic people are much more likely to get hired than people who simply match the job description.

4) Be Concise – None of the other 3 C's matter if you are not concise. Listen to the question that is asked and pause for a few seconds before answering it. Pay careful attention to the first question, as that is the one that sets the tone for the rest of the interview. Once you have finished answering it, stop. Do not offer answers to other things that come to your mind unless they DIRECTLY relate to the question. You answer should be short, sweet, and to the point. If you can weave in some statistics about your past performance, you'll hit a home run.

> **Absolutely Abby's Advice:** *Interviewing takes practice, but it is far less stressful when you truly know what you want your next job to look like. Interviewing for jobs that you love will be the easiest thing you'll ever do, and it will be easy for the hiring manager to make their decision to hire you also!*

▪ 75 ▪ Passion = Perfection

Passion can be your saving grace when interviewing against tough competitors.

Let's say that you're a hiring manager at a TV network and you are trying to choose between three qualified candidates for a receptionist position.

- Candidate A has 7 years of experience as a receptionist at a bank
- Candidate B has 3 years of experience as a receptionist at a medical device company
- Candidate C has 12 years of experience as a receptionist at a competing TV network

Who would you hire? The answer is the same at it frequently seems to be…it depends. Here is what it depends on for me…PASSION. The person that I want to hire is the one who wants to be hired more than anyone else who I have interviewed. Why? Because passionate people make the best employees.

The person who has been doing everything possible to get a foot in the door of the entertainment industry, and who lights up like a Christmas tree when I explain the job responsibilities, is the person I want to hire (assuming they are qualified for the role). That person is going to work harder than everyone else, be more motivated to succeed than everyone else, and will be more likely to build a home at my company for the next

3-5 years. Passionate people also tend to get promoted more quickly because they are drivers of their own success.

So, if each candidate presented themselves equally, and each appeared capable of performing the job well, I'd be inclined to select the one who seemed the most passionate about the position even though they might have less industry experience than the other candidates.

> ***Absolutely Abby's Advice:*** *Before your interview (and even before your phone screen), know the reasons why you are more excited than a cat chasing a mouse to have this job, in this company, and in this industry. Your passion will help you navigate your way through your interview, even if others before you are far more qualified. I promise you...it happens every day.*

▪ 76 ▪ Interviewing Boo-Boos

In my career, I have had the pleasure of interviewing many people at different levels for all kinds of positions. Even those who climb to the highest rungs on the corporate ladder still need to be sure they are aware of the interviewing pitfalls, and then avoid them at all costs.

Here are three interviewing boo-boos that applicants repeatedly make, whether they are intentional or not:

1) Do not bash your former managers – Even if your old boss resembled Attila the Hun or Shrek, you somehow need to find their redeeming qualities before your interview. Jog your memory a bit. Way down deep in the chasms of your mind, you can probably find something that you learned from your old boss, or accomplished with his or her help. If nothing else, you certainly learned how NOT to manage people, so you can have good feelings about that, although I would not mention that in your interview. Speaking negatively about your former boss may make

the interviewer believe that you might speak negatively about him or her in the future. This is not a career-enhancing plan.

2) Do not bash your former employers – Finding something positive to say about a company that laid you off after 15 years, without warning, will be tricky. Nonetheless, you Absolutely must find it. Think about all the skills that you learned and all the ways that you grew your career during your tenure. In other words, think of all the things you are grateful for. This positive attitude will go a long way in an interview.

3) Do not act desperate – Every interviewer knows that you are in their office because you want a job. At the same time, they want to hire people that have a strong interest in working at a job in their company and in their industry. When an interviewer asks a question and you respond with the words, "I have no problem with that", what they hear is, "I'll do it if I have to." Working should not be about desperation. It should be about passion. If you have "no problem" with many of the responsibilities of the job, it's not your ideal job, and thus, you probably will not receive an offer. Instead, search for jobs where you would answer questions with, "Yes, I would love to do that for you" or, "Yes, I would bring tons of value to that task" or, "Yes, I am the perfect person to fill that role for you." Keep in mind that you can't just say the words…you have to mean them. If you don't, we'll know.

> ***Absolutely Abby's Advice:*** *Becoming a strong interviewer requires lots of practice and persistence. Just trying to "wing it" is not going to help you score the most points. Now that you understand the interviewing boo-boos, apply an ouchless bandage to them so that they no longer stick.*

▪ 77 ▪ Touchy Topics

If hiring managers were being honest with you, they would tell you that on many occasions, they hire people who are similar to them, or people that they like. In order to be likable, you MUST develop rapport quickly with your interviewer. Talking about commonalities is important, but always beware of the touchy topics, which may take any rapport you had and throw it out the proverbial window.

1) Religion – Avoid bringing up religion as a conversation during your interview or making any religious remarks, no matter how minor they are. Even if the clues indicate that you are of the same religion, i.e., if the interviewer is wearing a necklace with a religious symbol, or if you notice a picture of a religious icon, you never know what might offend your interviewer.

2) Sports – Having small-talk conversation about the recent big game of the day is troublesome unless you are 100% sure that your interviewer roots for the same team. Imagine the sparks that may fly if you are a Yankee fan and your interviewer is a Red Sox fan. The safest bet is to avoid this topic at all costs.

3) Politics – Definitely avoid political conversations of any kind. Most people have distinct political views and you probably will not be aware of them until after you start working. During an interview is the wrong time to discover your differences.

4) Recreational Activities – Avoid talking about the event you attended over the weekend, especially if it suggests that you engage in excessive partying. Although your weekend activities are not any of your employer's concern, you always want them to think of you in a professional way.

5) Bad Weather – Even if you drove an hour in a combination of hail, rain, sleet, snow, and floods, do not complain about the

weather when you arrive. Your interviewer's goal is to hire people with positive energy. They don't want to hear that a simple thing like the weather is a challenge for you, especially when they have far more difficult challenges in store for you. And, you don't want them to think that weather will cause you to "call in sick".

> ***Absolutely Abby's Advice:*** *Touchy topics are just that… touchy. The more relaxed you feel, the more likely you are to bring up a topic that may be detrimental to your success. Sometimes these topics can be the kiss of death for your interview, if you choose wrong. Telling someone that you like the picture on their wall, or the knick-knack on their desk is typically a safe conversation starter. Avoid controversial topics until you have at least several weeks of employment under your belt, as a good first impression is a key to your success.*

▪ 78 ▪ The Dreaded Weakness Question

People say that there are no guarantees in life. Maybe so, but I guarantee that you are guaranteed to be asked a question in an interview about your weaknesses. Your goal should be to not just answer this question, but to answer it confidently.

Before I tackle the dreaded weaknesses question, let's first agree that no one is perfect, even your interviewer. The question is whether your particular imperfections are going to interfere with the specific job you are applying for.

An interviewer can ask the weakness question in a variety of ways:

1) Tell me Joe, what are your weaknesses?

2) Joe, what tasks are you most likely to procrastinate doing?

3) Joe, what skills do you wish you could take classes on?

4) Joe, in your last performance review, what came up for you in relation to your challenges?

5) Joe, if I called your former manager and asked him about your weaknesses, what would she tell me?

Start by creating a personal list of all of your weaknesses that could affect your job performance. Stick with this until you've come up with at least five true weaknesses. We'll return to this list in a moment.

It might be tempting to answer these questions with, "I am a workaholic so my weakness is that I have a hard time saying no" or, "I am a manager who has high expectations of my staff so I tend to push them too hard." Unfortunately, these are overused and any savvy interviewer will realize this. If your interviewer doesn't think you are being genuine, he or she will continue to press you until you reveal a weakness that is more believable.

Here is a real world example of a weakness: "I am a perfectionist. While that may not seem like a weakness, it causes me to put off finishing projects. To solve this problem, I typically ask my managers to give me deadlines so that I know when the project must be completed". Or, "I have been told that my presentation skills need some work, so I have asked for more opportunities to speak in front of groups and have recently joined Toastmasters."

So let's have a look now at that list you created. Did you list a weakness, which under the right circumstances can be also be considered an asset to a company? If so, offer that as an example. Then explore how you have overcome this weakness and how you are working to improve it. The key, as usual, is to know yourself – know what makes you a superstar and know what areas you need to work on.

Celebrating the fact that your interviewer did not uncover your weakness in an interview is dangerous. Wouldn't you rather be hired for your true self rather than trying to compensate for your weaknesses during your first few months when all eyes are upon you? I vote yes.

> **Absolutely Abby's Advice:** *Choosing a career where you can showcase your strengths rather than continuously trying to cover up your weaknesses is the ultimate goal. Being able to convey to an interviewer who you truly are as an employee and what you love to do will put you on the road to success.*

▪ 79 ▪ Are You Qualified to be Overqualified?

My mother gave me many gifts, but the best one she gave me was an excellent work ethic and passion for my career. My grandmother lived to be 95 and she worked until she was 94. If you think that I plan to retire when I'm 55, think again.

One year I received a call from a radio station in Ohio asking me to guest star on their job search segment entitled "Jobs For Candidates Over 50". This was an easy topic for me because as a recruiter, what I really care about is whether a person has the qualifications and the passion to succeed – their age has nothing to do with my opinion about them. If you believe your age is a problem, then it will be, simply because it will diminish your confidence, which spells disaster during an interview.

Regardless of your age, when you're on an interview, it's critical that you demonstrate that you are totally committed to, and interested in, the job that you are interviewing for. It is your responsibility to convince the recruiter that you are looking forward to making a home at their company for the next 3 – 5 years. It is your job to convince them that you have kept up with all the technology and terminology in your industry, and that you will fit in well with the team. Having a social media profile will help you prove your point. Most of all convince them that you have the skills that they are looking for, and that you are a mature, dedicated individual who takes responsibility seriously. And while you're at it, demonstrate an overabundance of energy and passion.

How many times after an interview do you feel like you hit the ball out of the park, only to receive a rejection letter in the mail? In how many of those cases do you wish that you knew the reason why someone wasn't interested in hiring you? My guess is that it's 100% of the time. Therefore, if someone ever tells you that you are "overqualified" during an interview, consider this is a blessing in disguise.

The fact is that these days, the majority of recruiters are reluctant to provide ANY feedback about why you didn't get the job, unless it's because someone was promoted or transferred into it, or unless the position was put on hold. It's difficult to provide honest feedback for a variety of reasons, so companies shy away from it.

When your interviewer actually tells you that the reason they are not interested in you because you are overqualified, start jumping up and down for joy (figuratively please…not literally). This news provides you with a chance to celebrate because NOW you have a chance to overcome their objection. It's Sales 101. You can only overcome something you know about.

After you have regained your composure from the excitement of being called overqualified, now it's time to tell them why they are COMPLETELY WRONG. This is of course assuming that they are, in fact, wrong.

Think about it for a moment. If you were hiring someone, would you want to hire a person who would be challenged by the responsibilities of your open position or bored by them in 3 months? Would you want to hire someone who could grow in the job or someone who might resign in a short while when a better offer comes along? These are silly questions, but I ask them to make a point.

141

It is your job to know why you are interviewing for this role. You know if you are overqualified long before you walk in the door. You don't need someone to tell you that. If you are honestly considering the position because you are looking for a lower level job with less pressure, that is a GREAT reason, and you should explain it in detail to your interviewer. If this is not your reason, try to find another good, and most importantly honest, reason for your interest.

In some cases you may choose to tackle your "overqualifiedness" before the interviewer mentions it as a sticking point, to avoid the proverbial elephant in the room. Remind them that your depth of experience means that you will accomplish more work in less time, and that the training curve will be shorter. Explain how perfectly your skills match their job description. Remind them of your specific accomplishments and how loyal you have been to past employers. And, remember to show your passion for the job, the company, and the industry.

Everything I've suggested above assumes that you are interested in the position you are interviewing for because you believe that you could truly be a value to the company in this role. However, if you are interviewing for a position beneath your skill level simply because you are desperate to find any job, a savvy interviewer will see right through your words and body language. If you truly are being honest with yourself, you will make the right decisions.

> ***Absolutely Abby's Advice:*** *Being called "overqualified" during a job interview is an objection that you can learn to overcome. Be thankful for this constructive comment from your interviewer. But, do be sure that the position you are applying for will in fact be one that you'll be passionate about for a long time to come.*

▪ 80 ▪ Skeletons in your Closet

Many jobseekers are concerned about explaining prior convictions, i.e., felonies or misdemeanors, during interviews. While the answer depends on many different factors, the good news is that like any other hurdle, a conviction can be overcome, when handled correctly.

There are a variety of factors that go into the decision each company makes about whether or not to hire you if you have a conviction. Some of these include the amount of time that has passed, the type of conviction, and the type of job you will be performing. Your success at being hired will also depend on the types of companies you apply to work at, as some companies tend to have more robust screening procedures than others.

If a recruiter asks you to fill out an application before the interview, read the criminal background check questions carefully. Most of the time, the question is "Have you been convicted of a crime?" If you have been convicted of any misdemeanor or felony, including driving convictions, your answer should be, "Yes". If you say no and the company discovers that you lied when they complete your background check, you will probably not be hired, no matter what the details of the conviction were. After all, lying on your application suggests that you will not be a trustworthy employee.

Some candidates may be tempted to answer, "No", and then take the risk that the company won't actually perform a background check. The problem with this approach is that if you manage to get hired anyway, you're still not out of the woods. Your new company might later implement a new background check policy that retroactively checks all previous hires. Do you really want this hanging over your head each and every day that you are working, or would you rather be hired by a company that knows about your mistakes and is willing to forgive them? Remember, the recruiter you are sitting with is a person too, and while

143

they may be bound by corporate policy, it might be more lenient than you think.

If you are ready to take the honest route, be prepared to respond verbally or in writing about the details of the conviction. Be honest about what happened and when it happened. Being honest about the conviction but not about the details will not help your cause.

Being honest about something you are not proud of will be difficult, but in my opinion, it's the way to go. I make similar recommendations to people who have been terminated from jobs. Explaining the situation and following it up with what you learned from the experience, in addition to explaining how you have corrected the behaviors, seems to be the best approach. We have all done things we are not proud of – it's the actions that we took afterwards and the lessons that we learned that really matter most.

When a company offers you a position, a good question to ask the Human Resources department is whether or not the conviction information will be given to your new manager, or whether it will remain confidential between you and the recruiter. Personally, I would rather not work for a company who would tell my supervisor about my conviction, because I would be concerned about being treated differently based on the information.

> **Absolutely Abby's Advice:** *Owning up to your past is something you need to get used to. Everyone has something in their background that makes them less than a stellar choice for a particular job or organization. If you keep at it, you will eventually find a company who will acknowledge your past history and be willing to hire you despite your blemish. Strive to be positive, professional, and polished so people will see past your skeletons.*

▪ 81 ▪ Asking Tough Questions

A jobseeker once asked me this question, "How can I ask difficult questions during an interview about a company's business model and performance, especially when the employer is receiving mediocre reviews from industry analysts?" The answer to this question is not necessarily straightforward.

During an interview, both parties are obviously on their best behavior. An interview is similar to a sales call. You are selling yourself to the company and the company is selling themselves to you. Both parties want to show their best sides and hide their weaknesses so that a mutually beneficial relationship can begin to develop. For that reason, you may think that asking difficult questions about mediocre company news is detrimental. Actually, ignoring the news and worrying about it later is far more detrimental.

The last thing that your interviewer wants to talk about is their bad press. However, in order for you to make an informed decision about the company, you need to know as much information about it as possible. The last thing you want to do is to look for a job a year from now when your new company lays off employees, including you. If you don't ask these difficult questions, you won't know the truth.

Then again, you may not hear the truth even if you do ask.

In many companies, employees are taught how to respond to specific bad press. If their stock price is declining, they are told how to explain it. If they recently changed CEO's, there is always a positive spin put on the story. If they had layoffs in the past few months, there are always reasons to explain the situation. Regardless, if you ask the questions, you should get closer to the truth about the answers than if you didn't ask.

For example, here are three ways that you can ask tough questions about earnings:

1) Can you please comment on the recent news about your 4th quarter earnings?

2) I read the recent news about your 4th quarter earnings. How does that impact you?

3) I read the recent news about your 4th quarter earnings. What is your opinion on that news?

Avoid asking any question that might make the interviewer defensive, such as questions that start with the word why. For example, "Why is your stock price going down?" or "Why should I consider working here when you stock price is going down?" And, before the interview is over, be sure that you also ask questions about the good news that you've read about so that you don't leave the impression that you're a negative person.

> *Absolutely Abby's Advice: Just because a company has bad press, it doesn't necessarily mean that you shouldn't work for them. There is no such thing as a perfect company as much as there's no such thing as a perfect candidate. Asking detailed questions about a company's performance is not only permissible – it's expected. To be able to make a sound decision, you need all the information available. These questions become part of the full package and will help you with your decision. So, ask away…but, just be sure to do it tactfully.*

▪ 82 ▪ Interviewing Your Next Boss

Many jobseekers believe that the sole purpose of an interview is to help a company decide whether or not to hire them. While that may be A purpose, a more important one is for YOU to decide whether or not to go work for the prospective boss.

How well you work with your boss is going to be a HUGE component of your success at your new company. Your boss determines your promotions, your raises, and also determines whether you continue to be employed at all. The boss has more power than you realize. Without chemistry in that relationship, you are most likely doomed. Many of you know exactly what I mean.

Some of you were hired by a company and soon after you started working, your boss changed assignments, or worse yet, companies. Sometimes this turns out to be a blessing and other times it's a curse, depending on the relationship that you develop with him or her.

In other cases, your boss remains the same, but similar to a relationship after a few weeks of dating, your boss' true colors come out. When that happens, you'll find yourself wishing that you would have asked certain questions to learn more about the boss BEFORE you accepted the offer? Here are several questions that you can ask the prospective boss during the interview:

1) How do you measure success?

2) What is your management style – more hands on or hands off?

3) What are some of your pet peeves?

4) How do you encourage your employees to grow?

5) How have you recognized your employees in the past?

6) What are the opportunities for cross training?

7) How do you reward performance?

8) What are your personal goals for the department?

9) If hired, how can I help you be more successful?

10) What has turnover been like in your department?

Some bosses are not going to appreciate being given the third degree, so if possible, scatter some of these questions during different parts of your interview. You can also ask other members of the interview team to help you answer the rest of the questions, in a tactful way. It may also behoove you to do some background checking on your boss much like what the boss is doing with you. If you can find someone who used to work for the boss, ask the person what it was truly like. Be careful about the questions you ask, as you don't know whom your new boss is friendly with.

It is critical that your boss' management style and your work style meld together well. Some bosses are direct and others beat around the bush. Some micromanage you while others let you sink or swim on your own. You will achieve much more success by choosing the right partner who may, in the right circumstances, later become your mentor.

Absolutely Abby's Advice: Finding the right match at work is nearly as important to your happiness as finding the right mate. Spend time searching for details about your new boss on Google and LinkedIn. You may learn some interesting facts about him or her that will help you say yay or nay. Notice the office vibe. Are people smiling and laughing or yelling and complaining? If your research and questioning points to nay, walk away. Or else, you may find yourself searching again sooner than you'd like to.

▪ 83 ▪ Food For Thought

An apple a day may keep the doctor away but it's one of the many foods you should avoid during an interview.

Interviewing for a job will rattle your nerves more than delivering a presentation in front of 10,000 of your peers. It is for that reason that I recommend you avoid any possible interactions with any of the five food groups during these stressful encounters.

A close friend of mine tells a story that literally takes the cake. He was interviewing a candidate who I'll call Steve for his first job out of college at a Fortune 500 company. After the interview, the hiring manager brought out a box of chocolate cake with five slices leftover from an earlier party. He asked Steve if he wanted some cake. Steve had been interviewing for several hours, and by this point, was craving something sweet and chocolate.

While you may expect this story to end with Steve's nice new suit covered in chocolate that is not exactly what happened. Steve must have been hungry because he took the entire box of cake, thanked the hiring manager and left. Needless to say, Steve wasn't invited back for further interviews.

Another food group to avoid during interviews is the warm beverage kind, e.g., coffee or tea. As enjoyable as it sounds to have a cup of caffeine with you as you stroll down the halls from interview to interview trying to stay awake, just think of how it will look when your coffee lands on your nice white shirt, your newly pressed pants, or on your interviewer. Stick with good old H_2O instead – at least it doesn't stain. Remember to bring your own bottle, in case no one offers one to you. Then, to be respectful, ask your interviewers if they mind if you drink it during the interview.

If you are invited to an interview over lunch or dinner, consider yourself lucky because you are clearly a top candidate. To practice for the interview, have dinner with a networking buddy and ask them to evaluate whether you are a neat eater, a closed-mouthed chewer, and a non-elbow-leaning conversationalist. Only if and when you have perfected the art of eating when under pressure, schedule the interview. Avoid ordering finger foods or anything where messiness comes into play. Also try not to over order or over eat. Take your cues from your interviewer.

> **Absolutely Abby's Advice:** *Interviews are stressful enough without having to concern yourself about eating proper portions from each of the five food groups. Eat a big meal beforehand, so that you are not even tempted to partake in items offered to you, some of which can lead to interviewing disasters. Then, when the interview is over, run to the nearest ice cream parlor and enjoy a heaping bowl with whipped cream and a cherry as you celebrate your successful day!*

▪ 84 ▪ Hurdles or Opportunities?

A jobseeker once asked me an interesting question. She said, "several years ago it seemed to be the norm to go through two or three rounds of interviews before an offer was made. Nowadays, it seems that the norm is four or five rounds. (a) Is this fairly common now? (b) Why is this? Are companies being extremely cautious now?" While these hurdles seem frustrating on the surface, you may find them to be just what you need for early success on the job.

When I first read the question, a smile came over my face as it evoked a memory from my own interviewing days back in the 90's. I had responded to an ad in the NY Times for a Recruiting Manager job at a prestigious New York City based company. From the ad, I knew that I had the perfect background for this job. I could tell from the ad that the culture was fast-paced and entrepreneurial, which was right up my alley.

The call came several days after I applied. I was ecstatic and looking forward to my interview. I went to the store and bought a new suit for the occasion. I was ready to play the interviewing game.

The first interview went perfectly. I connected well with the Director of Human Resources, my potential new boss. I answered everything as best as I could and I was sure this was going to be my new job. Before I had time to celebrate, he told me that I needed to come back to see the Vice President of Human Resources on another day.

I aced that interview too. Our personalities clicked. The job was mine…or so I thought. I was told that I had to come back to see someone else in Human Resources. And then I was told after that interview that there was another one. I ended up coming back for a total of 6 interviews on 6 different days. That meant 6 days of leaving early from work, 6 cab rides, 6 different suits, 6 different quick changes in the cab, and 6 days of being at the top of my game. I never complained. Eventually, I landed the job and enjoyed a long, satisfying career at the company.

Looking back, I realized that putting me through those hurdles was actually beneficial for both parties.

1) By the time I started, I knew that six people were on my side and because they approved of the hire, those same six people would want to help me succeed.

2) I had met six people – I knew what each of their goals were which meant that before I started, I knew what my goals should be in order to be successful in their eyes.

3) Rarely on your first day do you know the team you will be working with. Knowing six people reduced my first day anxiety tremendously.

4) Because these six people met me, they knew what my capabilities were and what projects they could give me early on. I had a huge jump start on day one.

Absolutely Abby's Advice: It's true that some companies are being pickier these days and asking candidates to prove themselves time and time again. Others have been picky from day one. The goal is for you to demonstrate your friendliness and flexibility at all times and NEVER act as if you are irritated with or impatient about their decisions, because that will take you out of the running faster than you can imagine. Instead, keep smiling and keep the stories you share during your interviews consistent. Most of all enjoy the journey. One day you will look back and smile about the hurdles you jumped through the way I am smiling now about mine.

▪ 85 ▪ Replaying Your Commercial

Thank you notes are the most underestimated steps of the job search process for a variety of reasons.

While you may look forward to receiving a thank you note from your best friend whose wedding party you were in, recruiters look forward to your thank you note for a very different reason. For us, they are a sneaky way to learn about the real you, your true spelling and grammar ability and your creativity shine through. Recruiters know that career coaches help candidates write their cover letters and resumes, but rarely does anyone seek advice for a thank you note. Having grammatical and spelling mistakes in a thank you note WILL cost you your job offer if the job requires those skills. The worst part is that you'll never know that that's what did you in, especially if you knocked them dead in the interview.

But…proving that you were not asleep in Grammar 101 is not enough. Your thank you note is a second chance to remind the hiring manager how ideal your background is for the open position he or she is considering you for. If you think of an interview as your commercial, your thank you note is your re-run. It is an opportunity for you to tell the hiring manager things that you may have neglected to mention while you were interviewing. It is your chance to provide examples of points you wanted to make that you didn't think of until after you left the building. It is your chance to mention some statistics about your performance that you could not extract from your brain while under stress. Above all…it is a chance to put yourself back on the hiring manager's radar screen.

Now, this does not mean that you should write a novel. Your thank you note should be short, sweet, and effective. You should write a different note to each person who interviewed you. I hear the groaning and the moaning, but trust me, it is well worth the little extra time. You wouldn't want your interview team to compare notes and discover that you didn't think your meeting with them was interesting enough to write about.

Your note doesn't have to be 100% different for each interviewer though. It can have some of the same opening and closing remarks as long as a majority of the note is different. The note should be personalized with details from your conversations with each specific interviewer. For example, you might say, "I enjoyed learning about the mermaids you are creating in your laboratory" or, "I enjoyed learning about the research you are conducting on space travel for dogs."

Always send a thank you note, regardless of whether you are interested in the position or not. You can send it by e-mail, snail mail, or the pony express. Just make sure that you send one. Leaving the relationship with the interviewer on good terms will always serve you well.

After you send the notes, exercise as much restraint as possible not to call or e-mail the hiring manager for at least one week. Then, one follow up or call will be fine. Delays happen and trying to rush the process may be detrimental to your success as a jobseeker. Having patience must be a part of your overall plan.

> ***Absolutely Abby's Advice:*** *As understated as you think the thank you note might be, I cannot overemphasize how vital it is to your success. Write your note and then proofread it like crazy. Then, re-read it again and perfect it. Your thank you note may just be the last piece of convincing your interviewer needs that you are the missing piece of the pie in his or her department.*

▪ 86 ▪ Start Your Own Fan Club

These days hiring managers will not hire you simply because you wore a tailored suit, handed them a polished resume, and answered their interview questions effectively. More and more these days, hiring managers and Human Resources departments want *proof* that you can actually do what you say you can do. That is, they want to speak to your greatest fans.

People have always been telling you to avoid burning your bridges when you leave a company. As much as it kills you to thank your obnoxious (substitute stingy, arrogant, misguided or smelly as you see fit) boss for the time you spent with him, you should do it anyway. It will serve you well in the future when the Human Resources representative from your new company calls to do a little bit of unofficial checking, when he miraculously discovers he's LinkedIn to your old boss. If you leave on good terms, your former boss will be less apt to tell your new boss what he really thinks of you.

Fans aren't good enough. You need raving fans. You need fans that are going to sing your praises and tell your new company that they would be crazy not to hire you. You need to dig up the skeletons from the past and remind them of the wonderful you.

The best plan is to call your former managers, one by one, and ask whether they will provide positive feedback to a prospective employer. If they say yes, give them details about the job, and then provide them with exact reasons why you would be perfect for it. Give them the ammunition they need to become a raving fan. Then tell them who will be calling and what their function is.

If your former manager says that they have a policy of not providing references, move on to someone else. Trying to convince them will not work, and honestly, it probably means they aren't one of your raving fans anyway. You know who the raving fans are. They rave because they were thrilled with your work and would do it regardless of being asked or prepped. Although, asking and prepping encourages them to rave promptly.

> ***Absolutely Abby's Advice:*** *If you have lost touch with your raving fans, use LinkedIn or Facebook to re-connect with them. And when you do, begin by apologizing for having lost touch. Nobody wants to be called every few years just for a favor, so make it a point to stay in touch with your fans starting today. Social media makes this simple as pie. Staying in touch will give your raving fans lots more to rave about the next time that you need them.*

▪ 87 ▪ Time is on your Side

Closing the deal on a job offer is like negotiating a good price on a car; that is, you should rarely accept on the spot, regardless of the economy.

The last car I bought was a red Mazda-3. I have always wanted a little sporty gem and finally it was my time to go buy one. The salesman went back to check with his manager as many times as you might be called in for more interview rounds. At the end of the day, the price was finally on the table. The offer was in my hands.

I looked at my husband and then at the car. I looked at the car and then my husband and then the car and then the salesman and then my husband, and then…I said what no one expected. "I'd like to think about it over night – will you be here tomorrow"? After spending half a day with me, the salesman was ready for this deal to be settled. I was not. I began to walk out the door, and his sales manager miraculously appeared. And then, suddenly the spoiler and the car alarm that I wanted were included in my price. I bought the car and continue to "zoom zoom zoom" around town.

In a down economy, your first instinct will be to say yes to whatever someone offers you. I'm here to tell you that in MANY cases, the offer is not their best offer. The fact is that if a company offers you a job, it's you that they want to hire, so your attempt to negotiate a better offer is expected, regardless of the economy.

The first step to a good negotiation is asking for more time. Instead of saying yes on the phone, ask if you can have 24 hours (or the weekend if it's a Friday) to consider it, regardless of whether you're planning to accept. Do not ask for too much time or the recruiter will know that this position is not your first choice. No one wants to hire someone who is settling or less than enthused about their opportunity.

The only reason to decide on the spot is if the company says it's now or never when you ask for the extra time. Then, you have a decision to make. Asking for time indicates to the company that there is more that they may have to do to convince you to take the job, i.e., more money, more benefits, etc. They will be thinking about their next move while you are thinking about yours.

During your extra 24 hours, determine if there are any other offers waiting in the wings. Now is the time to call the other companies you interviewed with to see if they are still interested, especially if one of them is your first choice. Having two or more offers gives you more leverage with both companies in addition to more power to negotiate. Taking an extra day to consider your options can also help you make better decisions about your future.

> *Absolutely Abby's Advice:* Delaying your acceptance of an offer for 24 hours gives you time to fully weigh your options. Spend the extra time thinking about the company, the industry, the boss, the hours, the commute, the benefits, the work/life balance, and most of all, the career opportunity. Remember though that there are lines of people behind you who will gladly take the job instead of you, so if you ask for too much extra time, your opportunity may vanish into thin air.

▪ 88 ▪ Salary Droppings

Many people have asked me how to make the decision to compromise and take a lower paying job, versus holding out for a more reasonable salary. The answer depends on your own individual situation. There are several different scenarios where stepping down a pay grade might make sense, but for specific and personal advice, your should consult your accountant or financial advisor.

Future Growth Opportunities

If you believe that taking a step back will offer you growth opportunities in that particular company, a salary cut may be something to consider. In other words, if you believe that you will not only be able to reclaim your former salary but also surpass it in short order, this is a risk that may very well be worth taking.

Changing Careers

Regardless of the economic climate, if you are changing professions or industries, you may have to take a step backwards either in salary or in title before you regain the career momentum you have been used to.

Career Passion

If you are ready to take a step towards finding your ideal job, you may decide to do whatever it takes to get your foot in the door. If the company you have always dreamed about working for is willing to hire you, even if that means you need to start out as their janitor, you might wish to consider it.

Competition

If you are searching for a job in a competitive market or in a competitive industry, you may consider taking a slightly lower salary just to be able to get to the finish line ahead of your competition.

Financial Difficulties

In some cases, you may feel that you have no choice other than to take a pay cut because you are in dire financial straits. Consider the option of finding temporary work just to keep you afloat. Then, when the ideal job comes your way, you'll still be available to pursue it. If you decide to take a major pay cut with the thought of looking again in the near future, you may have difficulty explaining to recruiters why you are leaving your new job so quickly.

> **Absolutely Abby's Advice:** *The decision to take a lower salary is rarely an easy one. If you lean in that direction, your goal should be to stick with your new decision for two or more years if possible. Adjusting your standard of living may help to make the lower salary palatable. Just remember that in many cases, excellent performance is rewarded with promotions and transfers. Whatever your new opportunity looks like, make every effort to be a superstar and you will soon be back to climbing the ladder of success.*

▪ 89 ▪ Negotiation Station

While each corporate recruiter's primary objective is to hire successful employees, they are also expected to protect their company's bottom line. This is why negotiations become complicated. You are trying to get the highest possible salary, and the recruiter is trying to save the company as much money as they can.

Once you receive an offer, the ball is in your court and you have the upper hand. The tables turn once you start the job, because you are strongly motivated to *keep* your job. Therefore, the best time to negotiate is during the offer phase.

Aside from salary, there are several other variables of your compensation and benefits package that may be negotiable.

If you ask for a higher offer and you are told that you have already been offered the maximum amount, consider asking for a six-month review instead. But, beware! The six-month review may lead you to believe that you will automatically earn more money in the future, once you have proven yourself. An employee who is a high performer will certainly have a better chance at earning a raise, but there is still no guarantee.

Thus, if you are promised a six-month review, ask if it is a six-month performance review or a six-month *salary* review. These are two completely different things. Anyone can promise a performance review in 6 months, 3 months, or 9 months but if the review is not tied to salary, you are less likely to earn more at least the end of your first year, especially if the company is struggling financially.

If you are a Director or above, you may be able to negotiate a sign-on bonus, which is typically paid as a lump sum over a short period of time. Sign-on bonuses are better than increased salary offers for employers because they are only a one time payment. Some companies also offer stock options to Directors and sometimes those are up for negotiation as well.

If the company doesn't seem willing to add financial incentives to your compensation package, consider asking for benefits such as additional vacation time. Many companies will not alter their benefits for individuals, but you won't know until you ask.

> ***Absolutely Abby's Advice:*** *The best time to negotiate is always when your foot is halfway in the door. Once your body is in the chair, you are no longer in the driver's seat. Ask and you just may receive!*

▪ 90 ▪   The Search is Over – NOT!

My friend Paul has dedicated his entire career to teaching autistic children. Like many other teachers who have the summer off, Paul was searching for a summer job. He interviewed for several positions and received an offer from one. Paul quickly accepted this offer and then called the other recruiters he was working with to let them know that he was no longer interested in continuing with their process.

A few days later, the recruiter that extended the offer to Paul called him to let him know that the company had just made the decision to eliminate his new position due to financial constraints. Paul quickly called the other recruiters he had been interviewing with, but they had already moved on to other candidates and, more importantly, were no longer interested.

Valuable lessons can be derived from Paul's experience.

When you receive a job offer, regardless of the economic climate, do not assume that your search is over. Continue to search until the end of your first week of employment. Company funds can be sliced right and left and reorganizations frequently happen at inopportune times. If your position is unexpectedly eliminated early on, you will want to be sure that your other options are still open.

> ***Absolutely Abby's Advice:*** *Stopping the clock when you receive an offer seems like the obvious thing to do. However, play it safe and keep your options open for a little while longer to be sure that you are standing on solid ground.*

▪ 91 ▪   Getting Back Into The Thick of Things

As exciting as going back to work after lots of downtime seems, it can also be a little bit of a daunting experience. It may even resemble your elementary school days – and I don't mean that you'll get to throw spitballs at the teacher. I do mean that you might feel nervous during the weeks leading up to your first day back in the game. There are many things you can do to make the transition less troubling.

As you prepare for your first day of work, thoroughly research the company's website and key players. You should be particularly interested in your new company's products, services, and culture. During the first few weeks, learning about the who, what, where, why and how is the main responsibility, so any head start you have will be helpful. You may want to find other people in your network (via LinkedIn for example) that can tactfully give you more information about the company and the key players.

If a larger company is employing you, you may want to ask if business cards and technology can be ready for your first day, so that you can begin to schedule meetings with key players in the organization when you arrive. Perhaps these meetings can even be scheduled ahead of time for you.

In some cases, you may be permitted to come in several days before your start date to set up your new workspace and to meet several members of your team. This will make the actual first day so much easier.

If you are feeling even a twinge of resistance when you ask these questions, it's time to retreat. The last thing you want is a reputation for being high maintenance before you even get there.

Consider re-reading the job description and the requirements for the job before your first day. You may already know what your first quarter goals are and if so, you can begin to develop your strategic plan and/or hone any skills that may be rusty.

Last but not least, before your first day, plan your commute and also your contingency plans in case of traffic. You don't want to be late on your first day.

> **Absolutely Abby's Advice:** *While everyone is nervous about going back to work, it's important that you believe you are prepared to handle whatever comes your way. Be excited about your new job but not so excited that you forget the importance of fitting in to the new culture. With your expertise, you'll be a superstar again in no time!*

▪ 92 ▪ First Day Jitters

One of these days, you'll finally be facing the first day of your new job. Starting a new job can be an exciting time for both you and your new manager, but can also stir up many emotions. Making a good first impression will help you avoid the need to make a course correction later.

Almost everyone who starts a new job, even at the most senior level, experiences the first week jitters. There are many people to meet, new lunch spots to discover and new water cooler gossipers to avoid. Here are some thoughts about ways to control these jitters.

1) Look for the Welcome Wagon – You know who these people are. They may not buy you a plant for your desk or fill your office with balloons, but these people befriend all new employees "just because". They may not be your best friend over time, but during the first week, they'll show you around as if they owned the place.

2) Dress the Part – On your first day, dressing one step above the crowd seems appropriate, as first impressions are important. Two steps up will make you appear to be trying too hard to impress the boss, so avoid wearing a 3-piece suit when everyone else is

wearing khakis. Arriving with a new portfolio is definitely acceptable regardless.

3) Find a Lunch Buddy – Asking someone at the same level in the organization (and ideally your same gender) to have lunch on day two or three is a great way to find an ally. Although it was easy in kindergarten, making friends is a bit daunting in the work place as egos and competition are at play. Taking the first step by asking someone to lunch is a great way to network.

4) Stop at Dunkin Donuts – Do you know anyone who doesn't appreciate a yummy donut, especially when it's free? I don't either. Bringing a box of Munchkins and leaving them on your desk will cause a flurry of people to stop by to "introduce themselves", although you and I will know why they are really there.

5) Don't be Afraid to Ask Questions – The saying goes that the only dumb question is the one you don't ask, especially during your first week when you're in training. Take lots and lots of notes about the 3 P's – people, processes, and policies while you are asking questions. No one will expect you to be an expert on your first day. Lay low and don't try to move mountains until you truly understand the big picture.

6) Remember Your Paperwork – In many cases, the Human Resources department will have sent you a large stack of forms to fill in and return to them on your first day. Remember to bring them along with your ID and proof of eligibility to work for your employer. Some employers will send you home if you forget your paperwork and that would be an embarrassment difficult to overcome.

7) Have Patience – If you find the first few days overwhelming, reassure yourself that once you establish a new routine, you'll feel right at home. If doubts arise as to whether or not you made the right choice, allow yourself five full days of work at your new job before developing any full-fledged opinions. A new job needs to stretch and challenge you in order for your career to grow. Don't be concerned if you feel awkward or out of sorts for a while like you felt during the first week of school. It's completely normal. Be kind to yourself and believe that after a few days in your new job you'll be ready to take on any challenges they can throw at you.

> **Absolutely Abby's Advice:** *Starting off at a new organization makes you want to make changes quickly to ensure success. However, tread lightly and make every attempt to fit in to the team and blend in with the culture. Many people and organizations find it difficult to accept change despite whether or not it will help them be more successful. The time will come for you to let your opinions be known, and you will sense when that is. Just like searching for a job, have patience and spend the time adapting to your new home. Then rev up your engine and enjoy the ride.*

▪ 93 ▪ Independent Thinking Day

In America we celebrate our Independence on July 4th, but since 1776, every day is really Independence Day. It is a privilege that we have the freedom to make choices of where to live, what to buy and what to eat – it is a privilege that many of us take for granted. Aside from having freedom in our lives, we also have freedom in our career choices, in how we search for a job, and how successful we are in it once we find it. It's all about thinking independently…or doing things differently than everyone else.

Independent thinking is the key to leadership. Leaders bring new products, new inventions, and new ideas to their organizations. Thinking outside the box and sharing it with others is the first step towards becoming a leader.

New jobs offer great opportunities to learn new skills – make a promise that you will try to learn something new about your industry or your job every week so that you can become more valuable to your employer.

Determine the skills that you are lacking that are preventing you from moving forward in your career. Then, find a way to acquire them while you have the time.

Everyone has a business idea inside of them. Perhaps this is the time for yours to emerge. Many of the most successful businesses were launched right after the Great Depression, so the economic conditions shouldn't matter.

Pay it forward. Help other people who are struggling with their search. Find a job search buddy and help make them successful.

Enthusiasm is contagious. If you start to see work as enjoyable, others will follow along. Positive energy creates happy employees and happy employees typically achieve far more than grumpy ones.

Networking is not just about job seeking – continue to build professional relationships outside the office even after you land to help you continue to grow your career.

Dare to be different than everyone else during your job search – think outside the box – find new ways to get recruiters to notice you.

Expect to be successful with your job search. Think positively each and every day. Success is just around the corner – you might be looking at it but you may just not be seeing it.

Notice what the most successful people in your company are doing, saying and wearing – ask one of them if you can pick their brain over lunch.

Celebrate the small successes. Set goals that you can achieve by breaking larger goals into smaller ones.

Encourage other people. If people at work are venting or complaining, make a conscious decision to act differently. Remind them of all the positive things in their environment and soon they will start to recognize them on their own.

> ***Absolutely Abby's Advice:*** *Appreciate the freedom that you have in your life, and in your job and in your career choices. Don't just act independently…think independently…and you will find your ultimate career dream right around the corner!*

The Emotional Side of Unemployment

▪ 94 ▪ Squashing the Job Search Blues

Finding ways to escape the job search blues is an important step in becoming a red-hot candidate.

Nothing is more important than having a positive attitude during your job search. Even if you aren't feeling your best, you have to learn to act as if you are. People are much more likely to help you (and possibly hire you) if you are emitting positive vibes rather than negative ones.

Think of all the people in your life who are grumpy, who have a glass half empty attitude or who like to complain about their troubles. Do you look forward to being with them for long periods of time? Are you still as friendly with them as you used to be? Do you rush to pick up the phone when they call? Do you tell them that you already have plans when they ask you to spend time with them? Now think about whether you would hire them if you had a job opening for them. If not, keep reading…

When you are in search of a job, it may be difficult to see the light at the end of the tunnel. Here are some things you can try. Different things will work for different people:

1) Join a gym, start walking or take up a new sport. The adrenaline that comes from exercise sends endorphins circulating throughout your body, causing an improved mood and general feeling of well-being.

2) Network, network, network – reengage with old friends and make new ones. Have coffee with everyone. Don't just join local in-transition groups but actively participate. Form small job search teams or find a job search buddy. You will find great comfort by hanging out with other people who are experiencing a

similar situation. Network in places where you will find employed people, such as your local Chamber of Commerce. You may even find one that wants to hire you.

3) Read books that deliver positive inspiration and leave you feeling like you are in charge of your own destiny. Two of my favorites are "Feel The Fear And Do It Anyway" and "The Secret".

4) Sign up for classes. Is there something that you've always wanted to learn but never had time? Is there a certification that would make you more marketable to an employer? Is there a weakness that could use some polishing?

5) Break the job search process into daily and monthly action items that are manageable. Don't just see landing a job as the ultimate success. Plan your search as if it was a project with deadlines and timelines. For example, celebrate when you have a phone screen scheduled or when you make one new networking connection. Keep a chart on your refrigerator like parents do for their kids so that your family can help cheer you on.

> ***Absolutely Abby's Advice:*** *Do not let yourself get down for long periods of time, as you will emit negative vibes when you are interviewing, and when you are meeting new people. Change your attitude and your outlook and only good things will come your way. Eventually you will find a wonderful job with people who truly appreciate your gifts. It is well worth waiting for!*

▪ 95 ▪ Don't Be a Bad News Bear

It never fails. When I'm speaking to a group of jobseekers, someone always asks me about the unemployment rate or about the state of the economy. My answer is always the same, regardless of how the question is asked and by whom. Your goal should be to focus on your search because that is unfortunately the only thing that you can control – unless of course you are the President of your country.

While the unemployment rate affects the number of jobs that are being posted, it does not affect how fast you land in comparison to your competition, because not everyone is on the same playing field.

Many of your peers are not differentiating themselves. Not everyone is networking, and many of those who are, may not be doing it effectively. Not everyone is using LinkedIn, Facebook, and Twitter. Not everyone is attending Chamber of Commerce meetings or sending out direct mail campaigns offering their skills to CEO's for part-time projects. Not everyone is signing up for temporary and contract work, and not everyone is thinking about starting a small business.

Some people go into a depression because of the economy but others find ways to make money other than by finding a job. Read the book "Cash in a Flash" by Robert G. Allen and Mark Victor Hansen and you'll understand what I am talking about. Being depressed is a choice, not an absolute.

The question is, if the unemployment rate was at 3%, would that mean that you instantly would find a job? No! If you can think of things to do differently that you should be doing, start doing those things NOW. Even if the unemployment rate rose to 15%, that still means that 85% of the population is employed. You only need to find one job. And as long as jobs continue to be posted, you can find it if you take the right course of action.

> ***Absolutely Abby's Advice:*** *Turn off your TV, avoid the newspapers, and focus on your own search. The jobseekers who land quickly despite the economy and the competition, are those who understand the true meaning of networking and those who are thinking way, way, way outside the box. Be one of those people and ignore the media. You'll be glad that you did!*

▪ 96 ▪ Recession Exceptions

According to Kipplingers, several industries tend to thrive in an economic downturn and continue to offer excellent opportunities for growth. When you think about why, it makes all the sense in the world:

1) Healthcare – Regardless of the economy, people unfortunately still get sick. You may even argue that stress unfortunately breeds more illness, which results in a need for more people to take care of them.

2) Entertainment – Because people are unemployed, and probably because they cannot spend money on as much travel, they tend to spend more money on movies, video games and sports. Entertainment also provides a great escape from the trials and tribulations of life.

3) Education – As people are unable to find jobs in their industry, many decide to return to college to complete or further their education. Community colleges typically thrive in a recession.

4) Retail Warehouses – Target & Wal*Mart have lower prices than typical department stores so shoppers are much more likely to shop there in a down economy. More shoppers = more jobs. Apply early for holiday positions at these stores and at department stores, as they tend to add helpers each year.

5) Accounting – Difficult times increase businesses' and individuals' desire to wisely account for every last dollar.

6) Repair Companies – It costs much less to repair something than it does to buy a newer version. It also costs less to do things yourself than to pay someone else to do it, so Home Depot may be another good choice for job leads.

7) Entrepreneurship – There are so many ways to make money if you have the motivation to work hard at something that you love doing. Some of the largest businesses still operating today were started during the Great Depression. Find a local SCORE Center (www.score.org) in your area, and speak with a counselor who is dedicated to educating entrepreneurs and small businesses throughout the United States.

> ***Absolutely Abby's Advice:*** *Choosing an industry that thrives in an economic downturn is a wonderful idea as long as you truly have a passion for it. Then, differentiate yourself from the rest of the pack and use your network to help find the needles in a haystack. If you are successful, you will soon be yelling, "Touchdown!"*

▪ 97 ▪   A Flock of Fears

Fear is defined in the dictionary as a distressing emotion aroused by impending danger, evil, pain, etc., regardless of whether the threat is real or imagined. Clearly, there are many fears associated with the job search process. The key is to overcome them one by one.

Here are some common fears that you might have along with some suggestions to overcome each:

Fear of making phone calls

Phone calls are important for many reasons. You might be calling recruiters, referrals, and prospective hiring managers to introduce yourself as a potential candidate. You might be calling interviewers to follow up a week or two after your interview. Finally, you might decide to call Human Resources departments to ask if they have received your resume. To avoid having your heart racing faster than the speed of light during these calls, remember that you are calling to offer them a solution to their current problem, and that solution is you. You are doing them a favor by filling a need they currently have. You are the solution they have been waiting for. It's just up to you to explain it to them concisely and coherently.

Fear of networking

It never fails. At every networking event I attend there is always someone standing on the sidelines watching, as if they are about to play a game of Twister with a bunch of people they don't know. Networking should be fun. It's about meeting new people, some of whom may even become new friends. Approaching people standing alone is the easiest way to begin to "work the room". To get started quickly, create three basic questions that you can ask a fellow networker at an event such as, "Where do you live?" or, "What do you think of this venue?" or, "Have you been to this event before?" These kinds of questions break the ice so that smooth sailing begins. Go to an event with the goal of meeting three people and helping them solve a problem or connecting them to someone they need. Inevitably, you'll find people who can help you as well.

Fear of being unqualified

Rarely, if ever, will you find a job that you are 100% perfectly qualified for. Just realizing this is a huge step in the right direction. This means that you are either overqualified or under-qualified for most jobs that you apply for. Does that mean you should not apply for them? Of course not! When a child makes a birthday list, do they receive everything on the list? Sometimes, but generally not. A wish list is just that – it's a list of what we wish we could get for our birthday and similarly, it's what we wish we could find in a candidate. Eventually we realize that there are no perfect candidates and we relax the requirements a bit. If you are at least 75% qualified for a job, there is Absolutely no reason why you should not apply. Ultimately, when you receive a call, you'll know that you're at least qualified enough to be considered. Be ready to explain why your other qualifications are strong enough to overcome the lack of skills that you are missing.

> **Absolutely Abby's Advice:** *The biggest fear we have to overcome, when we are searching, is the fear of rejection but unfortunately, it's all part of the game. You don't need every company to like you – you just need one. Before long, you will meet your match!*

▪ 98 ▪ Rejection Resilience

On one of my luckiest days, I was fortunate to cross paths with Mark Victor Hansen, one of the most accomplished authors of our time. Mark is the co-author with Jack Canfield of "Chicken Soup for the Soul", a #1 New York Times and USA Today bestselling series. I learned great lessons from Mark that day, the best one being how to develop resilience when it comes to rejection.

We have all been rejected on many occasions and for many different reasons. Two year olds are told that they can't stick their fingers in light sockets. Fifth graders receive C's on their book reports. Teenagers are told they can't go to parties without parental supervision. People who are dating are rejected way too often to mention. So then why does an interview rejection seem to hurt so much more?

Mark Victor Hansen told me that "Chicken Soup for the Soul" was rejected 51 times before a publisher agreed to publish it...51 times!!!! Anyone who has read even one of the Chicken Soup stories is probably as shocked as I was. Why on earth would even one person have rejected "Chicken Soup for the Soul"? And then 50 others?

I learned a similar lesson from my sales manager back in 1989. I can still hear his words as if we spoke yesterday. He taught me to think of my potential customers as if they were combined together in a funnel. Each time one customer says, "No", and drops out of your funnel, you celebrate because you are that much closer to getting to that "Yes". It is no different with job searching.

Rejections are not personal. There are many things behind the scenes that cause a company not to choose you, and you'll never know the reasons why. Many times, the reasons are far beyond your control. The thing to do is to prepare to the nth degree, present your best self, and go for it! If you receive a rejection, dust yourself off, and learn from your mistakes, if you think you made any. And then, MOVE ON without beating yourself up. Don't take rejection personally. Use it as a catapult to success.

> ***Absolutely Abby's Advice:*** *Eventually, you are going to find a job. It may take one more rejection, or ten – or maybe a few more. But, you WILL find a job if you persist and think outside the box. The goal is to accept the rejections you receive and keep going without quitting. Rejection is not failure. Giving up pursuing your dreams is the failure. Keep dreaming and you will get there. That's what happened to Mark Victor Hansen and that's what will happen to you.*

▪ 99 ▪ Unemployed With Children

A jobseeker once asked me how to discuss her continued unemployment with her children. As you might expect, there isn't a "one size fits all" answer to this question. The answer depends on many factors, including: the age and maturity of your kids, the kind of relationship you have with them, and the length of your expected unemployment.

Regardless of the reasons why you are unemployed, one thing is for sure – you MUST not let it get in the way of your confidence and self esteem. If your kids sense that you are worried about the future, they will start worrying too. But, if you paint the picture that things will get better soon, it should help ease their minds.

One mom that I know is using her current situation to teach her kids the value of money. She added chores to their repertoire so now they have to earn the things they want to buy. Another mom involved her kids with her job search by making it a project they could have fun with together.

Consider giving your younger kids the "gift of you". Spending time with them, when they are home from school and you would normally be working, is something special they will cherish. Baking cookies, going to the playground or the zoo, fixing something around the house together, sewing, finger painting, and having picnics are great sharing experiences. Remember that even though you may not be able to buy them material things right now, spending time with you is an invaluable gift.

It is a good idea to tell older kids that you need encouragement and support from them. Teaching them the difference between helpful and hurtful words is a good way to get them to understand the real you. These lessons will transfer nicely into interactions they will have as young adults.

> **Absolutely Abby's Advice:** *Being honest with your kids about your current situation seems to be the best practice, depending on their age. Giving them the opportunity to develop a better understanding of the world of work will be a wonderful lesson for them to use later in life. Reminding them that things will get better and asking them to help you stay positive will most likely be an excellent plan. Family matters and so do you.*

▪ 100 ▪ Your A-Team for Job Success

I'd like to share with you a few gems from an article written back in 2002 that still rings true today. This article reminds us that while losing a job can be a traumatic experience, whether it was planned or unplanned, we must stay positive and keep forging ahead.

This article, entitled "Steps to Take When You Lose Your Job", was written by Steve McCarthy, the President of McCarthy Strategies (www.mccarthystrategies.com). In the article Steve reminds us that while we may feel many emotions, including anger, depression, and frustration when we first lose our jobs, we should not allow our emotions to hinder our ability to search for a new job. In this article, Steve offers the reader several suggestions, which he calls the three R's: Rethink, Research and Reach Out.

I'd like to offer up some additional corresponding ideas that I've gathered from my experience working with the jobseekers over the years. I present to you the three A's: Asking, Answering, and being Absolute.

<u>Asking</u> good questions is an essential skill for all phases of the job search

1) Ask everyone you know if they are aware of any opportunities that might match your background. Ask them to let you know if any new opportunities come up in the future. Make a list of people to ask each week.

2) Ask questions about the company and the position during your interview. But...do your research first and develop a list of good questions before the interview so that you are prepared.

3) Ask other jobseekers what has been working for them and really listen to their answers. Then, be willing to expand your comfort zone enough to encompass new job search techniques.

<u>Answering</u> other people's questions succinctly is a highly valued skill.

1) Answering questions during an interview or a phone screen is obviously a skill worth perfecting. Remember that practice makes perfect.

2) Answer other jobseekers' calls for help. Not only is helping people extremely rewarding, but it's great to align with others who share your struggles. Determine what areas of the job search process you excel at and then teach other people your craft. Become a connector – connect people together who can help each other out.

Be <u>Absolute.</u> It's a state of mind.

1) Be someone who exudes confidence and is completely certain of what he or she wants. This is <u>your</u> job you are searching for. Taking the time to know yourself and know what you really want is of utmost importance in a job search. I've met people who put more thought into what kind of car they want to buy rather than thinking about what type of career will be the most satisfying for them.

> ***Absolutely Abby's Advice:*** *Ask and you shall receive. Answer and you shall succeed. Learn to speak the absolute truth about your ideal job and you will be a huge success!*

▪ 101 ▪ Sweeping the Sweepers and Keeping the Keepers

During your job search, there are many different kinds of people who you will connect with to help you reach your goals. Some will be welcome additions to your team who will help you rise to the challenge. Others will be uninvited guests who unintentionally sweep trouble into your life and potentially hamper your success. One key to your success will be to learn to differentiate between the Keepers and the Sweepers.

Keepers are the people who cheer you on, regardless of the choices that you make. These are the friends and family who believe in you whether you announce your choice to become a lawyer or a funeral director. They believe that the career decisions you make, no matter what they are, are right for you because you chose them. They are there to help you succeed and not to judge. These are wonderful people to have in your life and should be deeply appreciated, as you may discover them to be few and far between. Make it a priority to share all of your job search successes with them and enjoy the cheerleading that ensues.

When you are job hunting or considering a career change, a great person to add to your Keeper list is a former manager who believed you were an Absolute superstar when you were working for them. Even if you have lost touch with this person, he or she will still enjoy receiving an e-mail from you requesting their help in boosting your confidence. Ask them where you excelled and what your specific strengths were. Tell them what new goals you have, and ask them if they have any advice for you. Re-establishing ties provides an extra benefit in that you may also be able to ask them to act as a reference.

Job search buddies can also be excellent Keepers. These are people that you meet at in-transition groups who are conducting a similar search, even if it is for the same job in the same city. You can both cheer each other on and divide and conquer the job boards. You can mock interview each other and review each other's resumes. Two heads are better than one, and three or four turn you into a force to be reckoned with.

And then we have the Sweepers. These are the people who tell us how we should be living our lives, and are typically reminding us of the mistakes we are making. A Sweeper might say, "I told you not to take that job – I knew that you weren't cut out for it" or, "you should have worn a better suit for your interview" or, "starting a business is crazy – you'll never be able to make it work in this economy." Sound familiar? Having a Sweeper in your daily life can be detrimental to your job search, as he or she will slowly take little bites out of your confidence.

The good news about Sweepers is that sometimes they convey an important and grounded perspective. But unfortunately, Sweepers frequently confuse what is right for YOU with what THEY would do in your shoes. So don't avoid them completely, but carefully consider what they say and then consciously decide what advice to keep and what to throw away. Or, simply keep the Sweepers at bay until you have some great news about your new job to share with them.

> ***Absolutely Abby's Advice:*** *Find and attract as many Keepers as you can find. They will help keep you focused, on track, and motivated. They will also provide a "pick me up" when you are down. At the same time, make an effort to identify the people who are sweeping away your confidence and ask for encouragement instead. Soon you will be on a path to exponential success!*

Conclusion

I still remember, like it was yesterday, the day that I first realized that I wanted to write this book. Writing a book is a bizarre experience. You get to share your thoughts and feelings with the whole world, yet you never really know who is out there reading it and whether you truly are making a difference. As you write, you think you're going to run out of things to say but somehow, the words continue to flow. Writing each section of this book has taught me many lessons, many of which apply to job searching as well:

1) If you are an expert in some area, it's time to tell the world. Join networking groups and talk about your expertise. The world will appreciate you and will help pull you along your path to greatness.

2) Pay it forward. The more that you help the world, the more that the world helps you back. It seems like magic. All of a sudden the planets start aligning in your favor. Help your friends, help strangers, and especially help people who are less fortunate than you.

3) Keep at it. There will be days when you are down but you must keep going. You never know what wonderful surprise is lurking around the corner for you.

4) Say yes to success. Don't wait to celebrate until you've reached your goal, as it should always be a moving target. Instead, celebrate the small successes along the way.

5) Ignore the competition. It has nothing to do with you. Think outside the box. What are you good at? How can you serve people? What is the one missing thing that the world needs? Think of how you can fill that void and then go for it!

6) Be grateful for what is going well. Be grateful for breathing. Be grateful for your friends and family. Be grateful for your worldly possessions even if you'd like more of them. Be grateful for your health – don't take anything for granted.

7) Don't take rejection personally. Not everyone is going to like you or your work and not everyone is going to agree that you are a good fit for their job. Move on. It wasn't meant to be. When it is, it will happen.

8) Be open to coincidences. Is it a coincidence that three of my friends told me to see the same movie within a day of each other? Is it a coincidence that one of my friends met the Vice President of Human Resources of his favorite company while sitting on the stands at a Yankees game? I don't believe it is.

9) Ask for help when you need it. Searching for a job without asking for help is a disaster in the making. When you are sick, you go see a doctor. When your computer is broken, you take it in to a technician. When your career is broken, you need to invest in repairing it as well. If you've been out of work for a long time, there is a reason. You may or may not know what that reason is. But more likely than not, the personal "blinders" we all wear might be preventing you from seeing your own weaknesses that are slowing down your job search. Invest in yourself with someone who will help you take off your blinders and reach new heights. If you do that, you might just land faster, earn a higher salary, and have the best chance at finding a job that you love.

10) The world isn't perfect. Even if you wanted to write a top 10 list, you might only have 9 things to say. It's not perfect but it's perfectly fine. No job is perfect either, but it is well worth the effort to find one that is darn close.

In conclusion, believe in yourself and others will believe in you too. Have confidence in what you were put on this earth to do and find a way to do it regardless of how much money it pays. And then, get help finding it and doing it.

Looking forward to continuing to help you and one million other jobseekers with much appreciation and gratitude...I remain,

Absolutely Abby

Abby Kohut
President and Lead Consultant, Staffing Symphony, LLC
www.AbsolutelyAbby.com
www.CareerWakeUpCalls.com
akohut@staffingsymphony.com

Network with me at:
http://twitter.com/Absolutely_Abby
http://www.linkedin.com/in/abbykohut
http://facebook.com/abbykohut

Made in the USA
Charleston, SC
09 July 2010